YOU AND YOURS

Building Interpersonal Relationships

By
ELLEN McKAY TRIMMER

MOODY PRESS
CHICAGO

Library of Congress Catalog Card Number: 78-175498

ISBN: 0-8024-9820-5

Printed in the United States of America

This book is dedicated to my mother
who taught me my first and best lessons
in human relationships.

Acknowledgments

Scripture references from *The New Testament in Modern English,* translated by J. B. Phillips, copyright 1958, used by permission of The Macmillan Company.

Scripture references from the *Amplified Old Testament* used by permission of the Zondervan Publishing House.

Scripture references from the *Amplified New Testament* used by permission of the Lockman Foundation.

Scripture references from the *Revised Standard Version of the Bible,* copyrighted 1946 and 1952 by the Division of Christian Education of the National Council of the Churches of Christ in the U.S.A., used by permission.

Scripture references from the *New English Bible,* copyright by the Delegates of the Oxford University Press and the Syndics of the Cambridge University Press, 1961, 1970, reprinted by permission.

Quotations from *Introduction to Psychology* by Clifford Morgan, copyright 1956, used with permission by McGraw-Hill Book Company.

Quotations from *General Education in a Free Society* by the Harvard Committee, Harvard University Press, used by permission (world rights).

Quotations from *The Art of Loving* by Erich Fromm used by permission of Harper and Row, Publisher, Inc.

Quotations from *5,000 Quotations* by Henry C. Lewis, copyright 1945, used by permission of Doubleday and Company, Inc.

Quotations from *An Introduction to the Philosophy of Education* by Demiashkevitch, copyright 1935, used by permission of American Book Company.

Quotations from *Revolt of the Middle Aged Man* by Edmund Berglar, copyrighted 1957, used by permission of Hill and Wang, Inc., original publisher.

Quotations from an article entitled "Education Versus Western Civilization," in *American Scholar,* Spring, 1941, used by permission of the author, Walter B. Lippman.

Quotations from *The Ways and Power of Love* by Pitirim Sorokin, copyright 1954, used by permission of Beacon Press, Inc.

Quotations from *Marriage in the Modern World* by Phillip Polatin and Ellen Philtine, copyright 1964, used by permission of the authors through Lenninger Literary Agency, Inc.

Quotations from *The Ideal School* by B. B. Bogoslavsky, copyright 1936, used by permission of the author.

Quotations from *Making the Most of Marriage* by Paul Landis, copyright 1965, used by permission of Hawthorne Books, Inc., publishers.

Quotations from *Psychosocial Development of Children* by Irene M. Josselyn, copyright 1952, used by permission of the Family Service Association.

4

Contents

CHAPTER   PAGE

Preface   7

Part I

YOU

1. What Moves Me to Action?   11
2. Why Are My Actions Sometimes Evil?   15
3. How Can I Cope with Myself?   20
4. How Can I Change?   26

Part II

YOU AND YOUR SWEETHEART

5. I Think We Should Marry Because . . .   33
6. What Can I Expect from Marriage?   40
7. How Will I Know When I Find the Right Mate?   47
8. Give Us Your Best Wishes!   56

Part III

YOU AND YOUR MATE

9. Doesn't Marital Happiness Always Follow Love?   65
10. What Sexual Adjustment Will Be Necessary?   67
11. What Other Personal Differences Will
    We Discover?   72
12. What About Differences in Values?   77
13. Are In-laws Really Such a Problem?   85
14. Will Children Cement Our Marriage?   89
15. Will Relationships Outside the Family Cause
    Tension?   94
16. When Is a Marriage Counselor Necessary?   99
17. Does Marriage Improve with Age?   106

Part IV

YOU AND YOUR CHILDREN

18. We Have a New Baby!   113
19. Our Baby Is Growing Up!   119

20. What Does It Mean to "Train Up a Child"
     Physically, Mentally, and Spiritually?   123
21. What Does It Mean to "Train Up a Child"
     Socially?   130

Part V

YOU AND YOUR YOUNG PEOPLE

22. Are Teenagers Really Impossible?   141
23. What Are the Goals of Growing Up?   146
24. Are There More Goals of Growing Up?   151

Part VI

YOU AND YOUR PARENTAL FAMILY
RELATIONSHIPS

25. Life's Most Significant Influence—The
     Mother Relationship   159
26. Can You Help Me Understand My Parents?   164
27. Brothers! Sisters! Grandparents! What
     About Them?   170

Part VII

YOU AND OTHER RELATIONSHIPS

28. Are My Friends Really That Important?   175
29. How Can I Learn to Handle My Authority
     Relationships?   179
30. What Should My Church Relationships
     Mean to Me?   186
31. Should I Be an Influence on Contemporary
     Society?   190

Part VIII

YOU AND YOUR GOD

32. Does God Love *Me?*   199
33. What Is an Intimate Relationship with God Like?   204
     Notes   208
     Bibliography   214
     Index   220

Preface

FOR SOME YEARS NOW, I have been increasingly aware of the
need for Christian instruction in the principles of human relationships. The apostle Paul admonishes the older women (here
I qualify) to teach the younger women to "love their husbands"
and to "love their children."

Feeling this calling, I began speaking at many women's retreats, and at church and community groups on subjects pertain-
ing to family living. I found the need for counseling and instruction even greater than I had expected. Everywhere the comment
was, "If only I could get what I have heard to my family!" I
began giving an annual series of lectures to the women students
at Ontario Bible College, hoping that my students, many of
whom will marry ministers, could multiply my efforts in helping
families. Again came the comment, "Why can't we get these
lectures to the men students?"

Finally, the need for this book became evident. It contains
the result of fifteen years of informal study in psychology and
counseling, thirty-one years as a minister's wife counseling
church women, nine of these years also working as a probation
officer for the Ontario Provincial Probation Services, counseling
both men and women from the Criminal Courts of Metropolitan
Toronto. Added to this is the incomparable experience of being
married for thirty-one years and having raised two children of
my own.

I am greatly indebted to the many people both in the church
and out of it who have trusted me with their confidences. Any
individual cases described in this book are fictitious but are also
a composite of the experiences of people whom I have known

with similar problems. To all of these people I owe my greatest debt in the preparation of this book.

I also wish to thank Mrs. Kermit Ecklebarger for her help in typing and retyping the manuscript, and several other friends for reading and criticizing early drafts of the book. Throughout preparation of the manuscript, my husband, the Reverend Vincent Trimmer, has given me much encouragement and very helpful suggestions.

This book, written in everyday language, is not intended to be a scholarly treatise on either psychology or theology, although it touches upon both fields. It is a practical approach to the universal problems of people and their relationships. It is meant to help You and Yours.

Part I

YOU

1

What Moves Me to Action?

MODERN MAN'S DESIRE to answer the question of what moves him to action is evident in the popularity of books like *Games People Play* by Berne or *The Power of Positive Thinking* by Peale. Demand for the services of psychiatrists and mental health clinics also proves the urgency with which people are seeking self-understanding.

What makes us act as we do? Is there meaning in all behavior as psychiatrists tell us? Why do we feel compelled to act in ways we cannot fully explain? What motivates our behavior? Most of us admit that we act out of a desire to fulfill inner needs. These human needs can be classified as physiological, affiliative and status.

PHYSIOLOGICAL NEEDS

In the physiological area are the needs for food, drink, rest and shelter. Without satisfaction for these needs, tensions develop within us. Without food, a tension called hunger develops; without drink, thirst; without rest, tiredness; without shelter from the elements, feeling cold, hot or uncomfortable.

One other physiological need, more complex than the rest, is sex. Without food, drink, rest and shelter, the individual cannot survive long. These are individual needs. Sex is different—it is not necessary to the survival of the individual but only to the survival of the race. In his book *Introduction to Psychology* Clifford Morgan of Johns Hopkins University makes this clear: "Sex is a powerful motive, yet survival of the individual does not depend upon it in any sense."[1]

Some people charge God with giving us a need which *must*

11

be met and then denying its fulfillment by restricting the practice of sex to marriage. In light of Morgan's comment, this is not a valid complaint. However, sex is a need which, like other physiological needs, motivates our behavior. The full range of tensions which develop around *unmet* physiological needs are described as *appetites*.

AFFILIATIVE NEEDS

The second group of needs are those in the area of the *affections*. These affiliative drives include the need to love and be loved, to give and receive affection, companionship, understanding and sympathy. There is a sense in which sex can also be considered an affiliative need since it has both physical and psychological dimensions. Because these needs cause us to reach out to others and form relationships, they motivate our behavior as much as our physiological needs do. Just as youngsters run to quench their physical thirst at a picnic on a hot July afternoon, so people with unmet affiliative needs seek love. The more intense the hunger, the more compulsive the seeking. When needs are met, desire diminishes.

STATUS NEEDS

Status needs are the least understood. These include the need for recognition, accomplishment, acceptance, self-esteem, fulfillment and appreciation. Tensions that accompany them can be called ambitions.

Some interpreters of Christian truth confuse status needs with pride. God wants us to be humble but He also acknowledges the human need for status, for He tells us that if we humble ourselves before Him, He will exalt us.[2] Some Christians feel it is virtuous to grovel in self-depreciation, but Paul gives a better way: "I warn every one among you not to . . . have an exaggerated opinion of his own importance; but to rate his ability with sober judgment, each according to the degree of faith apportioned by God to him."[3] The golden rule also hints at the importance of self-acceptance: "You shall love your neighbor as *yourself.*"[4] Individuals who have no self-acceptance have difficulty in all their relationships. They cannot believe that others love them because their view of their own worth is distorted. Consequently they doubt the love of others and must constantly test those who profess to love them. This puts a strain on their relationships. Thus, distortion of the status needs hinders the fulfillment of the affiliative needs.

Self-acceptance is a healthy attitude based on ability to see and accept our own faults and weaknesses as well as our abilities and strengths. Regrettably, some Christians feel that if they do not despise themselves, they are obnoxious to God. Where does Paul fit into this picture when he says, "I have fought a good fight, I have finished my course, I have kept the faith: henceforth there is laid up for me a crown"?[5] Surely God would not talk of rewards if recognition and accomplishment were expressions of evil pride. Status drives are part of the human personality and are not evil unless they are directed against God. God wants to exalt us to a place of confidence, effectiveness and fruitfulness so we can live our lives in divinely directed success.

NEEDS ARE GOD'S GIFT

All our needs—physiological, affiliative and status—must be recognized as God-given and God-blessed. Denial of any of these needs results in personality distortion. When God created Adam and Eve, *He created them with physiological needs* and provided the perfect conditions of Eden to satisfy them—food to eat and a perfect place to live. *Also recognizing man's affiliative needs,* God said, "It is not good that man should be alone."[6] He made Eve to meet these needs on a human level, and He came to walk with Adam each evening to provide him with divine fellowship. *God provided for Adam's status needs* and placed him in charge of the garden where he named and cared for the animals and dressed the garden. He enjoyed a place of leadership which would have become an even greater responsibility as the earth became populated. God knew that the nature of His creatures required that they have worthwhile pursuits, recognition, responsibility and self-expression to satisfy their status needs.

All these God-given drives motivate our behavior; they are incentives to love, achieve, mate, learn, conform and communicate.

But why are my actions sometimes displeasing to myself, to others and to God if I am merely responding to my God-given needs? Is God the author of sin?

2

Why Are My Actions Sometimes Evil?

SOMETHING HAPPENED to the human personality when Eve sinned. God created her with normal needs, all met by His provision. Although her sin may seem trivial to the uninformed, it is not, for Eve doubted God's wisdom, questioned His love, and envied His position when she overstepped His one limit. She believed the lie that God was unwise in His restrictions, unkind in His denials, and unnecessarily rigid in His demands. Does this attitude sound familiar?

LUSTS ARE OUR PROBLEM

The day man first disobeyed God, greedy hungers were planted in his nature. These depraved motivations poisoned the springs of the human personality, and *lusts* rather than *needs* began to dictate man's behavior. *Lust* is a biblical term which, contrary to general opinion, is not restricted to sexual meanings but refers to any excessive longing or greedy hunger. *Lusts entered Eve's appetites*—she saw that the fruit was good for food and pleasant to the eyes, and she longed for it. *Lusts entered her affections* and she loved herself more than God. She determined to please herself and to involve Adam. *Lusts entered her ambitions* also and she yearned for a position equal with God. "If we experiment with the fruit we will be as gods, knowing good and evil" was her argument. Now the deception was complete, and greedy hungers permeated every area of the human personality —the appetites, the affections and the ambitions. Adam was not deceived, the Bible tells us.[1] He sinned because he could not refuse the pleadings of the woman he loved. Eve was deceived

15

into sin; Adam was persuaded into sin. The result—their physiological, affiliative and status needs were corrupted by lusts.

Sigmund Freud made no new discovery when he described the "id"—the seat of human impulses and desires. He pictured the id as clamoring for satisfaction against the control of the superego, which is similar to what the Bible calls the conscience.[2] One writer comments that Freud's id is "the bad boy of the personality." The heart is "deceitful above all things and desperately wicked," Jeremiah declared, and then asked, "Who can know it?"[3] "Knowing it" is the problem of psychoanalysis. It is man's attempt to probe the unconscious id to discover the motivations of behavior. Although human efforts to discover unconscious drives are admirable, they are limited. The Bible suggests that God alone can fully search the depths of the unconscious and discover its buried motivations: "Shall not God search this out? For he knoweth the secrets of the heart"[4] and "by him actions are weighed."[5]

Freud, because of his naturalistic philosophy, related the deep passions of the id to man's animal origin.[6] To him they were a hangover from man's evolutionary ascent. Disagreeing with this explanation of contemporay man's personality, the Bible teaches that the source of our evil impulses is not our animal ancestry but our Adamic ancestry. Paul declares that "by one man sin entered into the world."[7] The trouble began when our first parents allowed their appetites, affections and ambitions to be polluted with lusts. This is the age-old discussion as to the origin and nature of evil.

Jesus Christ also described man's evil acts as motivated from within: "There is nothing from without a man, that entering into him can defile him: but the things which come out of him, those are they that defile the man."[8]

James further describes the origins of temptation and sin: "Let no man say when he is tempted, I am tempted of God: for God cannot be tempted with evil, neither tempteth he any man: but every man is tempted *when he is drawn away of his own lusts,* and enticed [baited]. Then when lust hath conceived, it bringeth forth sin."[9] Our evil impulses motivate us to select certain stimuli from our environment, and the resulting conception from the union of inner lusts and outer stimuli gives birth to sin.

More recent theories of social scientists put less emphasis on unconscious motivations, leaning to the belief that man is the product of his social environment.[10] Some teach that he is a composite of the roles he plays in his social setting, and that his conflicts result from his inability to integrate his varied roles. This theory, the product of pragmatic thought, minimizes the fact that man is an individual self with opportunity and ability to select many of his own environmental influences. Environmental factors, therefore, cannot be considered as the full explanation of man's behavior. Man is not an animal conditioned by his environment, but a self led captive by his lusts. His lusts are so intertwined with his needs that often he confuses the two. Instead of being motivated by his God-given inner needs so that he seeks healthy physical, affiliative and status satisfactions, man is driven by his lusts which lead him into bondage to his greedy appetites, affections and ambitions. Lusts are not needs, but what some social scientists call "felt needs."

Sometimes one area of the personality is more lustful than others, which explains the diversity of sins. The Scriptures talk about "that sin which so readily (deftly and cleverly) clings to and entangles us."[11] Personalities driven by lusts in their *physical appetites* are prone to the sins of gluttony, laziness or sexual uncleanness. Others, led captive by the lusts in their *affections,* commit sin against their own natures after being persuaded into sin by a desperate desire to please a loved person, or perhaps by a longing to have exclusive love. This attitude fosters neurotic jealousy, envy, strife, and even murder. Other people, propelled into sin by lusts in their *ambitions,* are the "climbers" who are indifferent to others' needs and feelings. They are relatives of the Pharisees who plotted for Jesus' death. The Bible says that it was because of envy that He was delivered unto Pilate.[12] One Pharisee thanked God in the temple that he was "not as other men are, extortioners, unjust, adulterers."[13] Possibly he was completely unaware that the seeds of murder could have been planted already in the driving lusts of his ambitions. The Pharisees' lust for power gave them a burning passion to be recognized and praised. Such an attitude makes every other individual a competitor.

None of us is exempt from lusts which lead us into sin. We easily condone greedy hungers which produce the more socially acceptable sins, while condemning the bawdy lusts of the appetites. We justify lusts in our affections, since they masquerade as unselfish love, and we rationalize lusts in our ambitions because they promote us to places of leadership in the church. Who will know that our real motive is like that of Diotrephes, who loved the place of preeminence?[14] Status needs are healthy, but a lust for status is never satiated.

Indeed, one of the marked differences between a need and a lust is satiability. Needs, when met, are satisfied. Lusts are insatiably hungry and seem only to increase with feeding, which makes them the source of much human restlessness.

When there are lusts in different areas of our natures, conflict is generated between drives that cannot be integrated. Then there is fragmentation in the self, which gives the person a feeling of being pulled in two directions. For example, a man who has a lust for status will work compulsively. In so doing, he defeats the lusts in his affections which drive him to fill his wife's whole world. Unable to satisfy these two compulsions simultaneously, he is thrown into conflict which ends in frustration and anxiety.

THE HUMAN DILEMMA

This is the human dilemma—the corrupted springs of the personality, the motivations that man cannot control, which break forth in evil acts and result in guilt. How often I have witnessed the tears shed by a newly convicted criminal. "Why? Why did I do it?" he asks regretfully. We have all felt this remorse and guilt. Lady MacBeth dramatized it when she tried to wash the invisible blood of murder from her hands.[15] In her dreams, she was viewing the havoc created by her envy.

Paul confessed that he experienced the same downward pull within himself: "I do not understand my own actions—I am baffled, bewildered. I do not practise or accomplish what I wish, but I do the very thing that I loathe [which my moral instinct condemns]. O unhappy and pitiable and wretched man that I am! Who will release and deliver me from [the shackles of] this body of death?"[16]

It's a good question, Paul. Did you find the answer?

3

How Can I Cope with Myself?

THE HUMAN PROBLEM, then, is not, How can I cope with my environment? but, How can I cope with myself? Paul states it thus: "I will find it to be a law [of my being] that when I want to do what is right and good, evil is present with me and I am subject to its insistent demands."[1]

MODERN MAN'S ANSWER TO THE PROBLEM OF GOOD AND EVIL

The modern answer to Paul's conflict and ours is simple: Don't call anything "right" or "good." These are nasty words in our society, anyway. They have been replaced by words like appropriate, relevant, and socially acceptable. Recently a judge remarked to me that today people are either good or sick—never bad. He is concerned for justice based upon such a concept. In an earlier day, definite moral standards based on the Ten Commandments were upheld by the social conscience. This presented every man with a choice of right or wrong. There was an "ought to" in conflict with a "want to." If "want to" won out, guilt followed. Modern concepts replace the "ought to" with "what is best." Thus men set their own standards and, as Paul describes it, become a "law unto themselves."[2] This modern approach is aimed at removing the guilt which was supposedly produced by earlier "rigid" and "Puritanical" cultures. Today many assert that earlier cultures produced excessive guilt, resulting in mental illness, so they recommend greater moral freedom. But where is the soundness that was to have resulted from this permissiveness and moral freedom? Instead we see an increase in campus suicides, alcoholism, crime, drug addiction, and mental illness. And what group has the lowest rate of mental illness and delinquency? The Hutterite colonies, which are perhaps closest to the Puritans in their way of life.[3] Setting aside so-called outmoded standards does not solve the guilt problem because the law of God is written in man's heart.[4]

A few individuals can break moral standards and still seem free from guilt, but they possess a fearful detachment and emotional isolation bordering on psychopathy. An increasing number of them are being brought to doctors because of social failure. Usually they are diagnosed as sociopaths or as having a character disorder because they are disruptive in social relationships, in the home, the school, the place of employment, and in society in general. Recently a psychiatrist remarked, "Give me back the neurotic with his guilt and inhibitions rather than the character-disorder types I am seeing more and more in the last ten years." Sociopaths respond poorly to treatment because any relationship with them is difficult to form, and relationship is the tool of psychiatry and social work. Behavior therapy is the most recent approach to this problem. It is a system of punishments and rewards aimed at conditioning the sociopath to acceptable attitudes and behavior. Proper behavior is reinforced with rewards; unacceptable behavior is discouraged by penalties. This is really the process of normal child-raising. Often the sociopath has been raised in a too permissive home environment, which results in poor social adjustment.[5] On the other hand, the neurotic, who is sometimes the product of too rigid parental control, is an unhappy person, but not as socially disruptive as the sociopath. Despite the regrettable illness of the neurotic, many of them have made significant contributions to society.

RIGID CONTROL IS NOT THE ANSWER

Return to severe authoritarianism is not recommended. The Bible warns against this: "Fathers, do not provoke or irritate or fret your children—do not be hard on them or harass them; lest they become discouraged and sullen and morose and feel inferior and frustrated; do not break their spirit."[6] However, the same

Book says, "Correct thy son, and he shall give thee rest; yea, he shall give delight unto thy soul."[7] Correction means rewarding and encouraging acceptable behavior as well as punishing unacceptable behavior.

PAUL'S ANSWER TO MAN'S CONFLICT WITH EVIL IMPULSES

Removal of standards is not the answer; neither are rigid controls. Paul answers his own question: "Who will release and deliver me from the shackles of this body of death [speaking of his own evil impulses]?" His answer is, "Oh thank God!—He will! through Jesus Christ."[8] This can be our answer too.

Jesus Christ stepped into the human scene and, although He was God, He took a human personality wth human needs. He was tired, hungry, thirsty, and had human *appetites*. He loved and was loved; He had human *affections*. He had goals, and work to do, He learned, and labored and served God His Father and His fellowmen—He had human *ambitions*.

There was one difference. Like Adam before the fall, He had no lusts in His nature. On the mount of temptation Satan tempted Jesus Christ to sin. He was "in all points tempted like as we are [in His appetites, His affections, and His ambitions], yet [He was] without sin."[9]

JESUS CHRIST TEMPTED IN ALL POINTS

Gaunt after forty days' fasting, and full of a crying human need for food, Jesus could have fallen prey to Satan's suggestion that He turn stones into bread. But He refused, stating that God was the source of His "bread." Satan's attempt to plant lusts in His *appetites* failed.

Next, Satan appealed to His *affections,* requesting that He test God's love by casting Himself down from the pinnacle of the temple. Again Jesus refused, making it clear that His Father's love needed no testing: "You shall not tempt, test thoroughly or try exceedingly the Lord your God."[10] Satan could not involve Jesus in lusts of the *affections.*

The final temptation came in the area of His *ambitions.* Satan offered Him all the kingdoms of the world if He would acknowledge and worship him. Again He turned from receiving such a lust into His ambitions. His recognition and fulfillment would come from God the Father, and He wanted no shortcut to power at the cost of loyalty to His Father.

So our Saviour passed the tests which Adam failed. Satan failed in his attempts to poison the motivations of Jesus Christ's human personality.

CHRIST'S TRIAL AND CRUCIFIXION—A TOTAL DEPRIVATION OF HIS HUMAN NEEDS

In the experiences of Christ's trial and crucifixion, Satan attacked our Lord through every form of human need. It was of no avail, for He did not waver from His sacrificial purpose.

In Gethsemane, as He contemplated the cup of suffering that was before Him, Jesus suffered *physically.* He sweat as it were great drops of blood. From the agonizing conflict of the garden, He was arrested, bound, and dragged away to be tried by the seventy elders of Israel. Some spit in His face and buffeted Him, while others smote Him with the palms of their hands. This abuse went on until morning when Pilate's court convened. Before Pilate, the questioning began again. Pilate sent Him to Herod, and Herod back to Pilate, in the usual bureaucratic "passing of the buck." Next Pilate ordered His scourging and then turned Him over to the Jews for crucifixion. The soldiers took Him into the common hall where they jammed a crown of spikelike thorns upon His head, tore the beard from His face, and then sent Him staggering off down the road to Golgotha, carrying His cross. They goaded Him forward till He fell exhausted and bleeding in the torrid dust. They nailed Him to the cross and hoisted it aloft, tearing the sinews of His hands and feet. Ruthlessly the soldiers gambled for His robe. For hours He hung in the searing Palestinian heat. At last the sun was blacked out and darkness hid His agony. When He cried, "I thirst," they offered Him only vinegar and gall for His smarting lips. A chill settled over His naked body, ending in frigid death. No more physical deprivation was possible.

But this is not all. Our Lord suffered the denial of His *affiliative* needs. In the garden, while He agonized, His most intimate friends slept. Judas sold Him to the high priest for the price of a slave and identified Him with a kiss. In the judgment hall Peter swore that he had never known Christ. Finally His disciples all fled to safety, leaving Him to His tormentors. John alone came back to stand at the cross.

Jesus felt His mother's agony too as she stood at the cross. No doubt Joseph had died, for he was not there to comfort her. In His dying moments, Jesus gave her to the care of John. Now, deprived of every human relationship, He turned to His heavenly Father. He longed for a sense of His Father's presence, but heaven was closed to Him because He was bearing God's judgment upon our sin. He cried out in despair, "My God, my God, why hast thou forsaken me?" There was no one to comfort Him—God or man.

His *status* needs were equally unfulfilled. The hours of the trial were filled with humiliation, mocking, and slurs against His character. The mock crowning was a cruel prank against His claim to kingship, and the guessing game a ridicule of His omniscient deity. When the Jews were given a chance to release Christ, they chose the criminal Barabbas instead. Jesus they crucified with criminals who railed on Him because He claimed to be God and had not saved Himself and them. The rabble that gathered to watch His crucifixion reviled Him, wagging their heads and saying, "If thou be the Son of God, come down from the cross." The priests taunted Him, saying, "He saved others; himself he cannot save. . . . He trusted in God; let him deliver him now, if he will have him: for he said, I am the Son of God."[11] Worst of all was His Father's rejection. The earth convulsed at the sight of our Lord's humiliation.

THE ANSWER TO COPING WITH OURSELVES

Paul says this Jesus is the answer to man's dilemma of sin and guilt: "There is therefore now no condemnation to them which are in Christ Jesus."[12] John adds, "For God sent not his Son into the world to condemn the world; but that the world through him might be saved. He that believeth on him is not condemned."[13] "Who will . . . deliver me?" Paul asks, and then triumphantly answers, "O thank God!—He will!"[14] Jesus suffered all this and rose again from the dead to free us from our sinful selves. No wonder Paul said, "For to me life is Christ!"[15] Only in relationship with Him can we be set free from ourselves. There will be a tension in us as He helps us overcome our lusts —a dying, Paul calls it. In this dying are life and freedom—a resurrection to newness of life. It comes through total commitment to Jesus Christ.

4

How Can I Change?

SO FAR we have dealt with theory. Now let us apply this truth to lives.

HOW DID PETER CHANGE?

Peter learned the secret of change beside a fire on the shores of Galilee after a night of fishing. Watching Jesus in the fire-light, he thought of that other daybreak when he had placed his personal safety above his love for Jesus. He still felt the stinging curses on his lips, the look of disappointment from his denied Lord, the guilt which opened the fountain of his tears.

Now, by another fire, Jesus asked him, "Lovest thou me more than these?"[1] These? Did he mean the fish frying on the fire? An activist, Peter loved his food and his sleep and his comfort at the end of a night's work. Did he love Jesus more than the satisfaction of his physical *appetites?*

Or did the Saviour mean his friends—John, who took Peter to his home and shared the tears of his defeat? Or Andrew, his brother, who first brought him to Jesus? Steady, dependable Andrew, who, unlike Peter, held his words until he had something to say. The other disciples too. Did he love Jesus more than these? It was a hard question. Was Jesus first in his *affections?*

Or did Jesus mean the boat sloshing at the water's edge, now loaded with the night's catch? Peter remembered the sound of the sea slapping against the bow of his boat; the scent of fish, the pull of the nets, the sweaty bodies toiling in the half-light, the yell of night birds disturbed from their prey, the shimmer of moonlight sparkling on the slithering fish, and the comradeship of seamen banded together to conquer the elements. This was Peter's trade, his livelihood, his ambition. Did he love Jesus more than these?

"Thou knowest that I love thee," he answered. "More than these" was to come later, perhaps in the upper room. We do not hear him say it but he obviously did, sometime before his Pentecostal sermon. We know this because then he loved Jesus more than his own physical safety, more than friends and family, more than his trade. The Saviour got His answer—Peter enthroned God at the center of his life, God was in control at the center of his appetites, God's love was at the center of his affections, and God's will was at the center of his ambitions. This is the divine dynamic of change in the personality of people like us.

PEOPLE WITH GREEDY APPETITES

As long as there are lusts in the appetites of human beings, there will continue to be Esaus rashly selling the blessing of God for a full stomach—Samsons seduced to unfaithfulness by sexy Delilahs—Davids lured to sin with stolen Bathshebas—Mary Magdalenes controlled by their appetites. These people continue to repeat themselves in every strata of every society as they expend their lives in sensual pleasure. Stumbling from person to person to satisfy themselves, their emphasis is food and sex and pleasure and drinks and luxury living. Their sorrow is the cry of lives which their lusts have exploited. God wants to save such people from the lusts of their appetites, even as He saved Mary Magdalene, and to turn all the warmth of their sensual natures into loving others for Him.

PEOPLE WITH GREEDY AFFECTIONS

In every generation there are those who are driven by lusts in their affections. Hungry to be loved at any price, they are open invitations to exploitation, willing tools in the hands of the sensual or the ambitious. They comply without dissent to acts they loathe, and then withdraw in self-hatred.

Here stands Judas, exploited by smooth-talking priests because he wanted to be popular with the "in-group" and have his friends too. Lured into betrayal of Jesus, whom he may have expected to save Himself, his plan miscarried. When he returned in remorse to reverse his decision, the priests tossed him off like a worn garment. "What is that to us?" they yelled above the clink of the coins on the temple floor. "See thou to that." Reap your own bitterness and tears, Judas. How can we help it if your compromise plan failed?

The Samaritan woman craved love too, and tried to find it in a series of husbands. Disillusioned and escaping from the disdain of her neighbors, she met Jesus at the well. His love filled the vacuum at the center of her affections and ended her lifelong search.

Those with Greedy Ambitions

In every society there are Jacobs exploiting their Esaus with immediate gratification in exchange for lifelong advantage; the Pilates intent on power at the expense of people; the Zacchaeuses climbing to the place of advantage and raking in profits under the table; the rich men building their bigger barns and starving their little souls; the Cains murdering the Abels of their opposition; the forgiven debtors selling their neighbors into slavery for a pittance; the Diotrepheses loving their preeminence in the church and refusing the Johns a place, lest they capture center stage; the Pharisees who make long prayers in public and murder plans in private; the Salomes haggling over chief seats for their sons in the kingdom while the Saviour announced His death; the Sauls who are zealots for the wrong cause, persecuting the "right" minority. These are all still with us today— the people with the lustful ambitions who commit the socially acceptable sins.

Paul and Jacob and Zacchaeus all testify to the fact that these too can be changed by the grace of God—not by conformity to a set of rules but by the presence of God at the center of the personality.

Don't Be a Conformist—Be Transformed by God

"Be not conformed to this world,"[2] or as Phillips puts it, "Don't let the world around you squeeze you into its own mold."[3] The world referred to is not the world of nature but the world of people like the people we have talked about who are controlled by lustful appetites, affections and ambitions. In the same verse Paul urges us to give our whole selves to God and let Him transform us in the depths of our personalities: "Don't be a conformist acting out of outer pressures (even if they are religious pressures); be a non-conformist acting out of inner motivations resulting from the transforming work of God in your heart."

That's what happened to Paul, Peter, Jacob, Mary Magdalene, the woman at the well, John Newton, William Booth, the man who lives on your street who used to be an alcoholic, and the woman at work who cheated everyone until she met Jesus Christ. They were transformed. The word is *metamorphoo*—like the word used when describing the change that takes place in a caterpillar after he wraps himself into his cocoon. Giving himself to the power of God, he comes out a transformed creature fit for a higher form of living. He emerges as a thing of beauty and freedom because God has effected His purpose within him. This kind of inner change will express itself in all of our relationships.

"You" will affect "Yours," for the quality of the self determines the quality of relationship with other selves—your sweetheart, your mate, your children, your young people, your parents, grandparents, brothers and sisters, your friends, your authority figures, your church associates, and the society in which you move. All of these will feel the positive effects of the personal changes which God's love and grace can make in the innermost "You." The rest of this book is about these relationships.

Part II

YOU AND YOUR SWEETHEART

5

I Think We Should Marry Because . . .

ONE EVENING, when my son was five years old, I put him to bed and settled myself to enjoy the silence. Suddenly hearing loud wails coming from his bedroom, I ran to investigate.

"I don't want to get married," he sobbed.

"But you're just a little boy, you don't have to worry about that," I comforted.

"But I'll have to get married or be a tramp," he complained, "and I don't want to leave you and Daddy."

Then I remembered that, months before, while we were vacationing, we had seen a transient walking along the highway with his bundle of belongings tied to a stick. David asked about him, and someone in the car said, "He is a tramp." When he asked, "What is a tramp, Mommy?" we had explained that a tramp is a man who has no family. He does not work but wanders about the country, living on whatever people give him.

The matter was forgotten by everyone but David. He concluded from the conversation that there were two alternatives— to marry and have a family, or be a tramp. At five, both possibilities seemed frightening. He was comforted only by the example of his much-loved Sunday school teacher who had never married.

David was not ready for marriage because of age, but many who are old enough are not ready for other reasons. When David reached marriageable age, he seemed quite eager to leave his parents and live with the girl of his choice. It is interesting to examine what causes different people to marry. Some motivations are unhealthy. The following are a few of these:

"I'm Afraid of Remaining Single"

Some, like David with his two alternatives, feel that being single is unthinkable; therefore they marry prematurely or unwisely. Young women are more apt to marry for this reason than young men. Failing to consider the fact that being single is better than wishing you were, they marry to avoid the social stigma and teasing that come to single women over twenty-five. If they receive a proposal, they panic, thinking it will be their last. Decision under pressure is always unwise, and even more risky in a major choice like marriage. This kind of hurried choice is very common after an experience with a broken engagement which has shaken confidence in one's ability to attract and hold a person of the opposite sex. Beware of marriage on the basis of fear of being left without a life partner.

"I'm Pregnant"

Pregnancy is a poor reason to marry, but it is often behind such a choice. Soon such mates are seeking help for a sick relationship because such "unions of expediency" are risky.

If a single girl becomes pregnant, she should be helped to decide objectively whether her only interest in marriage is to solve her immediate problem, or whether the father of her expected child would, under other conditions, be her marital choice. This decision is difficult, if not impossible, in the midst of hysterical comments such as "What will people think?" "I told you so!" "Why would you do this to your parents?" or "You should have known better!" Young people need parental support and acceptance more than ever before at a time like this. If the girl decides that she does not want to marry the baby's father, she will need help to plan for her child's future.

There is no easy solution to the problems of a girl who is about to become the mother of a baby whose father is not a suitable marriage partner. She must cope with parental and community pressures, her own guilt, and often financial inability. Her own immaturity will make the situation even more difficult for her.

If she decides to place her baby for adoption, her parents can be a comfort and support during her stay in a home for unwed mothers and in the lonely guilt-ridden days following the birth. It is important that parents not allow their own subjective feelings to hinder them in offering this help. There is no painless solution, but there can be a sharing in the pain. One mistake is never solved by another. Premarital pregnancy with its resulting problems is not helped by parental rejection.

If the young couple love each other and seem motivated to marry, quite apart from the pregnancy, and if, in the opinion of both sets of parents, the union appears to have potential for success, marriage may be the solution. In one such case, a seventeen-year-old couple, both still in high school, married and the four parents nursed the marriage along to maturity. The girl lived with her parents, fully supported by them. After the birth of the child, her mother cared for the baby while the girl returned to school. The fellow lived with his parents and continued school, fully supported by them. He worked at a part-time job and contributed weekly to the support of his child. The couple spent each weekend together, alternating between their parents' homes. Only after they both finished school and the young man found suitable employment did they move with their child into an apartment of their own. Even then, the parents gave frequent baby-sitting services so the young people could have adequate social outlets without too much expense. When they seemed ready, they were given full responsibility and independence from both sets of parents.

"I'M UNHAPPY, AND ANYTHING IS BETTER THAN THIS"

No one should marry to get away from something, but often this decision is made on the flimsy reasoning of escapism. Perhaps there is marital conflict, drunkenness, financial stress, or lack of warm communication in a young person's home. The decision to marry, then, is made because of the availability of a mate rather than his suitability—he is the symbol of escape from a difficult situation. The choice is a reaction rather than an action. And, too often the unpleasant home situation is repeated in the new marriage.

Then there is the lonely young person who hopes to find happiness in the married state. This person will soon find that a wedding ceremony does not melt loneliness, discontent, and personal conflict like spring snow. Instead, the added pressures and responsibilities of marriage and parenthood may intensify the original unhappiness. Discontent is often caused by an inability or unwillingness to face life, and marriage is no cure for this. Each mate must make his own contribution to marital happiness.

If an unhappy person chooses a happy mate, he will subject him to overdoses of bad temper, depression, discontent, touchiness and pessimism until resentment develops in the previously happy mate. This resentment will poison the relationship and clog communication.

This does not indicate that both partners in a marriage must be bubbling, optimistic extroverts. Often a person of this nature is attracted to a serious, introverted person who will be less expressive, but not necessarily less happy.

If you are thinking of marrying an unhappy person, don't expect to be a reformer. Your mate's unhappiness will affect the marital relationship more than the marital relationship will affect his unhappiness. If you cannot accept your intended mate as he is *now,* marriage is unwise.

"I Find It Difficult to Control My Sexual Urges"

If marriage only involved sexual compatibility, this motive might be valid. But marriage is more than an exercise in mating. Therefore, sexual appeal is not the only criteria for choosing a mate.

Paul did say, "It is better to marry than to burn [with ungratified desire]," but this statement does not imply that a mate is merely a sexual object.[1] The statement is an answer to a question asked by the Corinthians—whether it is better to marry or to remain single. Making it clear that this depends on the individual, he said, "It is well—good, advantageous, expedient and wholesome for them [the unmarried] to remain [single]."[2] He made it equally clear that for some it is better to marry. The choice is to be based on their individual needs, including their need for sexual release. He noted that some cannot cope with the sexual restraint needed to live as a single person, while others are unable to adjust to marriage. The whole question here is—to marry or not to marry?

Suppose you have decided you are the kind of person who should marry. Paul says to you, "Learn to take a wife [or husband] for yourself from pure and honourable motives, not to gratify your passions."[3] He is talking now about deciding who and when to marry. He says, don't let sexual passions make these decisions for you. To marry a person merely for the satisfaction of your sexual urges, he implies, is both immoral and dishonorable. This is not the proper motive for mate choice.

One of the causes of such a sexually pressured choice is premarital petting and the accompanying fear of indulging in premarital intercourse. Such a conflict rules out careful consideration of all the other factors which are important in deciding to marry a person.

This does not mean that physical attraction between the mates, which after marriage will be expressed in sexual intimacies, is unimportant. It is certainly one of the factors which must be considered in mate choice.

"I FEEL SORRY FOR HIM BECAUSE HE HAS NEVER HAD ANYONE WHO REALLY LOVED HIM"

It would be hard to estimate how many sick marriages are founded on pity. We have all observed ill-mated couples—the clever, efficient husband with the scatterbrained, ignorant wife; the socially well-adjusted wife with the socially inadequate or hostile husband; the woman of integrity and refinement married to a crude and insensitive husband. In many of these apparently mismated unions the element of pity has been a significant factor.

Pity does not produce a marriage of autonomous equals, but a marriage of incompatible opposites. Feeling sorry for a person and desiring to help him are not love. Instead of being helped by such a marriage, the inferior mate is placed in a position of unfavorable comparison for the remainder of his life. Mentally, socially, morally or culturally, he is living in a different world than his partner. He is more likely to restrict his pitying mate than to change himself. When change fails to materialize, bitterness and regret are the result. Then the mates will move back into their own separate worlds, even though they may continue to live under the same roof.

It is never safe to marry because of pity. Offer your acceptance and encouragement, but look elsewhere for your mate.

"I Need Someone to Take Care of Me"

No woman is wise to contract marriage with a mate who makes no effort to accept his responsibilities as a provider; yet, to marry for financial security alone is to marry for the wrong motive.

It is surprising how many women, faced with a choice between two prospective mates, will be influenced too much by a fat bankroll or a status position. Often a poor man can offer the gifts of love, congeniality, helpfulness and understanding which are more important than material riches. Besides, a study of the relationship between marital happiness and financial stability indicates that happily married people are more likely to succeed financially than the unhappily married.[4] So even if there is a temporary financial struggle, a happy couple will undoubtedly succeed financially later in life.

I have talked to girls who decided to marry because they were sick of getting up early to go to work. They remarked how nice it would be when they were married and away from the "grind." The young men who marry these girls will find themselves with more than their share of responsibility, for marriage is no escape from responsibility; it is a relationship where each mate carries his share of the load. Some marriages look like the Bible description of the ox and the ass yoked together. The one member of the team chafes under the unequal yoke.

Some young people marry to avoid personal responsibility. I have known young men whose mothers call them several times each morning to get them to work on time. When I asked one youth how he expected to be independent as long as this situation remained, he remarked that when he married, his wife would have to be responsible for making him get up. I have known other men who depend on their wives to earn the living. No young man should enter marriage with these attitudes.

All of these motivations for marriage spell trouble later. They indicate unrealistic expectations. What can a person expect from marriage?

6

What Can I Expect from Marriage?

PEOPLE DIFFER GREATLY in their interpretations of what they should find in a marriage relationship. Some have unrealistic expectations which doom the union to failure before it starts. What should a person expect from marriage?

A university professor from Louisville, John Scott Long, used the following formula to rate a girl: physical attractiveness, 40 percent; cooking, 15 percent; skill with money, 15 percent; sewing ability, 5 percent; health, 15 percent; similarity of interests, 10 percent. His values and priorities appear to be distorted. I would like to suggest the following realistic expectations and allow you to set them in order of importance according to your own personal tastes:

COMPANIONSHIP

Women today seem to rate companionship high on their list of expectations. A common complaint from dissatisfied wives is: "He never shares anything with me" or "He never talks." A marriage partner should be a good friend as well as a lover, for many marriages shrivel into routine niceties because there is no mutual sharing of experiences, no mutual communication of the emotional life.

These are things that a mate has a right to expect from marriage and which partners who really love each other will cultivate more and more as the years pass. Eventually there will seem to be communication even in their silences.

AFFECTION

Another expectation in marriage is physical response. People vary a great deal in their ability to give affection, but every mate has a right to some tangible expression of love. A person who highly values this physcial side of love should not choose a mate who is not expressive. Each partner needs to learn to interpret the meaning and depth of the other's expression and to know when the other craves affection.

RECOGNITION

Recognition is a realistic expectation in marriage. Often this need is not understood but, if unmet, it becomes the source of vague discomfort. A husband may say, "My wife always makes me feel like a nobody." A wife may say, "I don't feel comfortable at a social event with my husband." Such remarks indicate a lack of ego-building recognition.

If a mate is overcritical, belittling or even indifferent, this tragic deterioration can happen in a marriage. Men, because of the drain on their egos in the competitive world of business, need the encouragement of their wives. Women need recognition to keep them from feeling like a convenience for their families, or a buffer for everyone's bad moods. The warm encouragement of an understanding mate is insurance against these strains of competitive business or the pressure of mothering.

Few people are consciously aware of recognition, and fewer still know how to give it. Wives think they are filling this need when they say, "But my husband knows how much I appreciate the way he supports his family and is helpful around the house!" Husbands think their wives are satisfied with a certain unspoken contentment which they feel when observing their wives' housekeeping or mothering efforts. Recognition is not merely appreciating what a person does. It is admiring a person for what he is—a unique individual different from all others with his own strengths, weaknesses and desires. Recognition in this sense is expressed almost unconsciously in many little ways—an admiring look, an encouraging comment, a reassuring pat, a thoughtful act. In essence, it is the gift of freedom to be oneself—a necessity in all successful relationships.

Often when recognition is lacking in a marital relationship it is a mutual problem. Each mate craves approval, and neither is able to give it. Some people have grown up in a home where they have received little recognition and therefore have narrowed, fragile egos. These individuals need more recognition than others, but all of us have a right to expect recognition from our mates.

SEXUAL SATISFACTION

Sexual satisfaction is also to be expected from marriage unless the conditions which would satisfy a mate are extremely excessive or perverted and cannot be met by the partner. If so, professional help should be sought. There needs to be flexibility in meeting this need as well as a willingness to be understanding at times when a mate is emotionally drained or physically ill. A thoughtful partner will need to restrain his desires temporarily at such times, but an understanding mate will not expect more than reasonable restraint.

PARENTHOOD

Parenthood can be expected in marriage, although no one should marry for this reason alone. Unless there are health reasons prohibiting it, every mate has a right to expect that eventually his partner will want children in the marriage. To refuse this indefinitely, unless it has been agreed upon during courtship, is not fair to one's partner. The Bible tells us that children are a heritage of the Lord.[1] To avoid parenthood unnecessarily is not fair to one's mate. The use of contraceptives to delay or limit the coming of children is a personal matter and should be decided by the partners themselves. It is necessary in deciding this to take into consideration whether the motives behind such a decision are selfish and materialistic. Sometimes mates who began to practice birth control because their two incomes were temporarily needed to establish a home, have extended their delay to include all sorts of nonessential purchases. This can go on for years, until the standard of living becomes so high that it will always require two incomes to maintain it. All this

time, one of the mates may be unhappy because of an unfulfilled desire for children.

Some couples are childless although they wanted to have
children. If this happens, every effort should be made to find
the reason. Often it is purely psychological and can be corrected
by taking a more relaxed attitude. Sometimes when a couple is
willing to accept the fact that they may not become parents, a
pregnancy takes place. This phenomenon is frequently observed
in the case of couples who give up hope and adopt a child, only
to find within a few months that they are about to have a child
of their own. Sometimes working with children in the church
gives a certain satisfaction to childless couples.

People without children should be very sure of their motives
before adopting a child. Although parenthood is a fulfilling
experience, children should not be adopted merely to satisfy a
parent's emotional needs. Sometimes childless couples, although
not adopting children, make significant contributions to children of others through means of the extra time and money available to them in being childless. Again, it is a personal matter
which must be decided after prayerful consideration.

Under normal conditions a mate has a right to expect children
from a marriage and should not be denied this right except for
reasons of physical or mental illness.

SECURITY

Security is something which a wife has a right to expect from
her husband. Love wears a little thin when it is not supported
by material provision. Eric Fromm in his book *The Art of Loving* makes "care" one of the qualities of love.[2] If a man really
loves a woman he will do his best to provide for her, not
squandering needed funds on his own luxuries or failing to
maintain employment.

A wife should not only expect security but appreciate it when
it is given. A considerate wife will not spend more than her
husband can afford but will live within their means so that he
will experience success in providing for her. Until I began to

counsel men I was not fully aware of how concerned they are about providing for their families. I discovered that a normal male's feelings of adequacy are deeply rooted in his success in this area. If a man does not try to support his wife he is lacking in mature love for her. The Scriptures indicate that if a man does not provide for his family he is worse than an infidel.[3]

A man also has a right to expect security from his wife. She meets his need for security by providing a home environment where his physical and emotional needs are met. No matter how frustrating a day has been, the husband who comes home to a contented wife and a good meal finds security. There is a great deal of truth in the old adage, "The way to a man's heart is through his stomach." A husband is justified in expecting an attractive house, good meals, laundry service, and the many other things that make a well-organized home. If a wife works, by mutual agreement with her husband, he should be more helpful around the home and not expect the same amount of efficiency. However, the wife will still be the homemaker and should keep this in mind when she decides to work. In general, a mother with children is needed at home except during school hours. A husband should be spared concern over children who are not properly cared for. Unless dire circumstances make it necessary, it seems unwise for a wife to work during her family's early childhood years. There are exceptions to every rule and perhaps with a good mother substitute or nursery school a mother can work without damage to her children when this is necessary. No matter what the situation, both mates should find security in marriage.

"I Hear that Marriage Isn't All Sunshine!"

No young person goes into marriage realistically who does not have some *negative* expectations.

"Will I Lose Some of My Freedom?"

It is sensible to expect some loss of freedom in marriage, and this will increase with the coming of children. No two lives can be intertwined in a partnership without some "give and take," but sometimes young men and women expect to be as free after marriage as before. Even after children arrive they feel no ties. Until they are ready to accept home responsibilities they should not marry, because if they do they will be sorry later. The fact that their activities are church-related does not change the responsibility.

I asked a sixteen-year-old who had been in serious trouble in the courts, "How do you get along with your father?" "Fine," she replied. "I never see him. He's at church every night." God never intended our service in the church to crowd out our service in the home. These should be balanced well. Even church workers sometimes fail to accept a necessary loss of personal freedom and independence in marriage.

"Will I Have to Delay or Forfeit Some of My Dreams?"

Sometimes marriage brings a temporary loss of self-realization and ego satisfaction. During the early years of child-rearing, a young mother will prehaps feel unfulfilled unless she is the kind of person who finds the care of infants very satisfying. Peculiar as it may seem to men, all women don't. A husband will also be wise to curtail his activities during this period in order to give emotional support to his wife and to help her during these demanding years. The years of children's dependency are short compared to our modern life expectancy, and this part of our lives can be very rewarding if it is dedicated to parenthood. Many years of life are left for other kinds of self-realization which will be all the more enjoyable if we have done a good job of raising our children.

"Will We Have Some Quarrels?"

Differences and quarrels are to be expected in any marriage in which both mates are individuals. Most people don't want to marry a "blob" who has no opinion and no selfhood. Sharp differences of opinion will occur at times, and each mate should be free to explain his viewpoint. If an issue can be discussed without heat, this is mature and admirable; but if some anger is generated, it should not be considered as a sign of marital breakdown. The Bible does not say, "Don't be angry." It says, "*Be ye angry*, and sin not: let not the sun go down upon your wrath."[4] Anger becomes sinful when it is harbored in the heart in the form of malice and resentment. It is better to discuss differences than to go quietly about with a heart full of resentment, for such bitterness hurts a marriage much more than a marital spat that blows over in a few moments. In the midst of such disagreements there is communication. As time goes by, this kind of disagreement will lessen. Hundreds of minor adjustments will emerge into an overall pattern of marital adjustment.

To expect harmony in marriage at all times is unrealistic and leads to an inhibiting of feelings and a clogging of the lines of communication. Honesty is the only basis for healthy relationships, and it should not be sacrificed to avoid conflict. Silence when honest communication is needed is a form of dishonesty. God anticipated differences between marriage partners, otherwise He would not have bothered to identify the husband as the source of final authority when there is an unresolved disagreement.

Since expectations with which we enter marriage affect our later adjustment, it is very important in preparing for marriage that a young person establish realistic expectations. They are important tools with which to build a happy relationship.

7

How Will I Know When I Find the Right Mate?

HAVING DETERMINED that your motivations to marry are healthy and your expectations in marriage realistic, you will be looking for a suitable partner. Perhaps several persons of the opposite sex will attract you, but that alone is not enough. The person you choose must also have the qualities to meet your expectations. To marry a charming but irresponsible person, when security is high on your priority list, is folly. To marry a person who is physically attractive but has never had an original thought, when you place great importance on mental sharing, is accepting defeat before the race begins. To marry a sloppy but congenial mate when you highly value neatness is to court frustration.

When young people ask a happily married person, "How will I be sure when I have found the right mate?" most married people will answer, "I don't know *how* you will know, but you *will* know."

This answer sounds to the unmarried like a useless piece of advice; but, when these same people are happily married, they will realize that it is the nearest one can come to answering the question. What people are trying to say when they give this answer is that there will come a deep awareness of belonging together. You should be looking for a relationship which creates this awareness.

Webster defines marriage as a "close union." Paul describes the human personality as spirit, soul and body, for man is a trinity like his Maker.[1] So, if marriage is to be a "close union" it must be a union of two personalities—spirit, soul and body—

47

in a common bond. Yet, neither person loses his own individual identity. As you date casually and then more steadily you will become aware of this developing union if you have found a suitable partner.

Spiritual Union

The spirit is that part of us which can know God and comprehend spiritual truth. When sin entered into the human race, man died spiritually; he no longer communed with God, and his spirit became inoperative. Therefore, a person with no spiritual life relates only on two levels—the soul and the body. If a person knows God and has been made alive by the Holy Spirit, he can relate on three levels, so then spiritual compatibility must be considered in his choice of a mate.

When mates relate spiritually they have mutual communion with God and share the understanding which God gives to each of them. If a person knows God, then, it is very important that he choose a mate who can share this part of his life, otherwise there will be a whole area of incompatibility in the relationship. Since the spiritual has a decided effect on the emotional, moral, mental, and physical life, spiritual incompatibility may spill over into other areas and affect compatibility there. This is why there cannot be a complete union of the whole individual with his mate when a believer marries an unbeliever.

Marriage partners who have a close union spiritually as well as emotionally and physically have an extra dimension which gives greater cohesiveness to the marriage. In his book *Making the Most of Marriage,* Paul Landis has a chapter on "Religion in Mate Choice." While all religious people are certainly not Christian or spiritually alive, yet findings of several American sociologists have indicated a positive association between religiousness and success in marriage. Landis suggests that perhaps this is because religion is a great socializing factor: "It is particularly shocking for the person whose life is built around religious values to realize, after marriage, that the person whom he has married is entirely without religious orientation and

holds none of the concepts and values which make life meaningful to him."[2] This gulf of spiritual incompatibility widens
with the coming of children.

Landis goes on to say, "A study by Zimmerman and Cer-
vantes of 40,000 urban families with children found that divorce rates are three times as high in mixed marriages [where
mates do not share the same religious beliefs]." He also notes
that a study of the parents of 6,500 schoolchildren in Spokane,
Washington, showed that 24 percent of the marriages ended
in divorce when there was no religion involved, as compared
with a 17.4 percent divorce rate in religious homes, even though
the parents were of mixed religion. Lewis Terman in his study
of 792 California couples reveals that there is a significant relationship between religious training and high marital happiness scores.[3]

A truly Christian person, then, who knows and loves God
through Jesus Christ, will look for a mate who can have a close
spiritual union with him. This adds the strength of divine help
to the marriage. This side of the union should develop during
the courting period.

SOUL UNION

There must be a "close union" of souls in a successful marriage. The soul is that part of man which feels, thinks and
decides—his emotions, mind and will. During the courting
period a "close union" will develop in this area also, so that
there will be an awareness of compatibility in the emotional
responses of each mate to the other. Feelings of affection, comfort, security and contentment will develop whenever they are
together. There will also be a mental response of each mate to
the other—a deep sharing of the thought life. The couple will
share their ideas on subjects important to their marriage, such
as money, sex roles, in-laws, children and birth control. They
will find that they have common motivations toward similar
goals, and that their ideals and philosophies of life are similar.
The Bible reveals the importance of this when it asks the ques-

tion, "Can two walk together, except they be agreed?"[4] As time passes they will become increasingly aware that they are deeply united in their emotions, their thought life, and their goals and purposes. This kind of closeness cannot develop if every date is either a necking session or a whirl of activity. There must be occasions when young people take time to know each other through hours of talking together during leisurely walks or quiet dinner dates.

PHYSICAL UNION—DESIRED BUT NOT FULFILLED

Besides spiritual union and soul union, both mates will have a desire for physical union—a deep longing to be "one" and to give themselves physically to each other. In the Christian view, this longing should not be fulfilled until after marriage. There will be expressions of deep affection between the couple, especially during engagement, but these should not include any act directed toward sexual climax. Petting is the prelude to intercourse and in the Christian view should be reserved for marriage. Some Christian young people who practice sexual intimacies which excite them almost beyond control, rationalize such practices by saying that they have not proceeded to sexual intercourse. They seem intent on placing themselves under as much sexual pressure as they can without tipping the scale beyond the limit of intercourse. No wonder their relationship develops irritability and petty quarrels.

The Bible refers to this kind of rationalization when it tells us that we "should abstain and shrink from all sexual vice; that each one of you should know how to possess [control, manage] his own body (in purity, separated from things profane, and) in consecration and honor, not [to be used] in the passion of lust." The passage then goes on to say that no person should "transgress, and overreach his brother and defraud him in this matter."[5] This indicates that a person should not only control his own sexual urges but help others do the same. It is a warning against the common dating practice of petting which excites beyond the place where one can control sexual urges.

The word "overreach" in this passage means to overextend oneself beyond one's rights, and to overpower. It is also used of exerting a stronger personality upon a weaker one, sapping it of its individuality so that the person is controlled rather than acting according to his own wishes. Sometimes a Christian girl on a date with a sexually aggressive young man will be so skillfully excited sexually that she will act in a way she would not have believed possible for her, with her kind of convictions about premarital sexual activity. The behavior which this young man produced in his girl was done by overreaching—overpowering her by excessive sexual excitement. Conversely, a girl on a date may seduce a young man who has every desire to abstain from premarital sex activity so that he becomes sexually aggressive. Then she may stop him just short of intercourse—this is defrauding him (the other practice warned against in the verse). She has aroused him sexually and then cheated him out of the satisfaction of the desires she has aroused. She should not have made a toy of his sexual feelings in this way. Neither of these practices is fitting for Christian young people, even when they are engaged.

In his recent book, *Marriage in the Modern World,* Phillip Polatin, professor of psychiatry at the College of Physicians and Surgeons of Columbia Unversity, points out the damage caused by the practice of premarital sex against one's conscience. Even though the book takes no moral stand, it states, "Contrary to some popular fears, sexual abstinence is not harmful. It may be uncomfortable, but it is far less harmful than are the anxiety and conflict which guilt-ridden people suffer about [pre-marital] sex."[6]

In a study by Kirkendall it was found that pre-marital intercourse usually weakens and sometimes terminates an engagement relationship.[7] Another researcher, E. E. LeMasters, finds that sex (both intercourse and petting to orgasm) before marriage tends to gloss over serious differences between couples so that they do not appear until after marriage.[8] William Reevy, writing in *Marriage and Family Living,* after a study on marriage predictability, states, "The group with unfavorable marital predictions can be characterized as being more active sexually than the group with favorable marital predictions."[9] Landis states that the works of four other researchers (Locke, Terman, Davis and Popenoe) indicate that virginity prior to marriage is most favorable to *total* marriage success.[10] Even the Kinsey Report, which has done much to encourage premarital sex, admits that those who have had premarital sex are much more likely to have extramarital relations.[11] A study by Hillman of inquiries brought to an advice column of a metropolitan newspaper, indicates that premarital sexual intercourse had brought more problems to the column than any other single factor.[12]

These facts may help to explain that while the union of spirit and soul should develop before marriage, the physical side of the union is for after the wedding. Then there will be no concern about going too far, and the Christian couple will be able to give themselves physically to each other with an abandon and joy not possible outside of marriage. They will be glad they have waited so that their first experience of sexual intimacy can be fully enjoyed, rather than ending in frustration and guilt. Books on the subject by Dr. Evelyn Duvall and others expand this viewpoint.[13]

If a deep spiritual union develops between two Christian young people and their souls are drawn together in a close union of thought life, emotional life and goals, and if they feel physically attracted to each other, then they will know that they have found their life partner. Only the marriage will be necessary to make it possible for them to complete their "close union." Then "they two shall be one flesh."[14] Some today are saying, "Why is a wedding important? It is just a formality." A wedding is a vow before God and a group of witnesses that the bride and groom are making a lifelong commitment of themselves to each other. To the serious and responsible it is an important event—after which they are prepared to give themselves fully.

This is the pattern of Christian mate choice. How much

better it is than the concept of premarital sex experimentation which brings to the marriage memories of sexual intimacies with other people in other places.

RESPECT IS IMPORTANT TOO

When I was in my late teens an elderly Jewish friend of our family visited our home frequently for lengthy periods. During one of these visits she noticed that I was dating casually. She seemed concerned, perhaps because she was raised in an Eastern culture and was suspicious of our Western methods of mate choice. One evening she drew me aside and said, "Never marry a man whom you cannot respect, even if you feel greatly attracted to him." To my Western mind this seemed like a peculiar emphasis, and I paid little attention at the time. However, the thought did remain in my mind because, having no living grandmothers, I considered this woman the voice of her generation. I respected her wisdom and trusted her motives in giving advice.

Now I know through experience and study that she was right. Romantic feelings cannot be trusted exclusively in mate choice. Fromm identifies "respect" as one of the four important ingredients of love.[15] Although his description of respect carries meanings well beyond the insights of my elderly friend, her concept of love turned out to be much more accurate than mine had been. Now that I too am a grandmother, I cringe, as she did then, when I hear teenagers being fed our Hollywood concept of love. Their transistor radios instruct them constantly about love, as if it were an irresistible and uncontrollable mania which leads inevitably and immediately to bed. If the feelings of romance are produced by a worthy person, good. If not, then one must proceed anyway, because escape from "love" is as impossible as escape from smallpox. I find that many of the disillusioned victims of such nonsense escape from their romantic feelings soon after they settle down to face the realities of marriage. As my friend warned, there must be respect for the individual one chooses as a mate. This is especially true when we accept the Christian view of the family.

GIRLS ARE CHOOSING A HUSBAND AS WELL AS A MATE

Is there a difference between a husband and a mate? Yes. In the Christian family the husband has the place of final authority in the home. In a compatible union this authority may seldom be used because the mates can communicate well and reach agreement on issues to be decided. However, there are times in every marriage when a husband and wife will reach a deadlock on some matter. Then the husband must use his God-given authority and make the decision for the two of them. Whether a husband is a Christian or not, he should be given his rightful place as the head of his home. The Bible which says a husband should "love his wife as [being in a sense] his very own self," also says, "Let the wife see that she respects and reverences her husband—that she notices him, regards him, honors him, prefers him, venerates and esteems him; and that she defers to him, praises him, and loves and admires him exceedingly."[16] Does this verse bring you up short, girls? Think about it in the light of the young man you are now considering.

YOU ARE CHOOSING A PARENT FOR YOUR CHILDREN

Few young people consider the fact that they are considering a parent for their children when they are in the process of mate choice. This is just another reason why the person you decide to marry should be a respected person—as he is—and not a candidate for a starry-eyed mate's reform program.

Can this person be trusted to discipline and train my future children? Would I be happy if my children absorbed the attitudes, values and ideals of my present "steady?" Will my children be proud someday to say "This is my dad" or "This is my mom"? These are questions worth asking when choosing a mate.

Perhaps I have made clearer the answer to the question, "How can I know for sure when I meet the right person?" You will *know*—except during the week of your wedding. It is not at all uncommon during the few days preceding the wedding for young people to develop severe doubts and fears about their mate choice. This is merely a panic state which should be ignored if one has been quite sure of his choice until that time. Several times in my experience responsible young women who have made a very careful choice after a fairly lengthy courtship have expressed these doubts. Now they are happily married, and the richness and depth of their family life are evidence that their last-minute doubts were merely a case of pre-wedding jitters.

8

Give Us Your Best Wishes!

WEDDING WISHES TO THE GROOM

SOON YOU WILL BE the forgotten man at your own wedding. You won't mind though. You will be grateful to your bride for stealing most of the attention. Otherwise the quaver in your voice, the trembling of your hands, and the dampness on your brow will announce that you are apprehensive about becoming a husband. You are wondering if you will be able to meet the needs of this girl whom you love. Will you find the demands of marriage greater than your ability—socially, financially and physically? Let me add my hopes to your fears.

I hope your wife is not a spendthrift. A wife who soaks up a man's money like a sponge will sap the spirit from the most ambitious husband. However, I would not want you to be "stuck" for life with an extreme economist whose appearance will advertise to the public that the ends are just not meeting. Nothing will make a man feel more like a failure than a wife whose wardrobe resembles yesterday's salad. I hope when you step out with your girl a year from now, you will think she is as pretty as before you married her. Not only because she has made an effort to be that way, but because you love her more.

You don't just want an attractive wife, I'm sure. You want a good cook, but remember that good cooks are the product of appreciative eaters. However, I hope you will not expect her to kill you with kindness, which too many wives are doing these days. Don't complain if she limits the number of pies and cakes she bakes. Yours is a wise wife if she keeps your diet simple. You will appreciate this virtue when you reach fifty and are still feeling fit after eighteen holes of golf.

I hope your wife will be a good mother yet not be completely absorbed in motherhood. Youngsters have a way of robbing a woman of herself if she lets them. May your wife find ways to preserve her own individuality so that your children, instead of growing into demanding little monsters, will have a healthy regard for the rights of others. By understanding early that no relationship in life should completely monopolize a person, they will come to see that their mother is not living entirely to serve them, or to be a clearing house for their problems and complaints. They will realize that she is a person, with problems, needs and desires of her own. They will expect her to follow her own pursuits and, when they become older, they will appreciate her outside interests.

Above all else, I hope your wife will not let your children rob that part of her that belongs to you. A man feels like a third party on a date with some women—they are all mother. If your wife is this kind, she will feel guilty every time she leaves the children with a "sitter" to go out with you. Every evening when you return from work you will find her so completely drained by her children's unreasonable demands that she has nothing left for you. The children in such a home are better fed, better rested, better read, and better entertained than their mothers. They grow up thinking that the world turns on the axis of their desires. I hope your wife will let your children shoulder some of her load early in life. It will put respect and unselfishness into their natures and prepare them for healthier adult relationships. They will make good marriage partners.

I have another wish for you. I hope your wife will grow with you. Nothing is more pathetic than to see one marriage partner progress mentally and socially while the other remains stagnant. This stagnation happens more often with wives than with husbands. May your wife read and listen and get out among people, thus keeping her mental and social development in pace with her chronological age. Otherwise you will find yourself lost for conversation on evenings at home and reluctant to take your wife into certain circles. May this not happen to your marriage. I want you to always be proud when you say, "I would like you to meet my wife."

May the girl you marry not be a *housewife,* as she will be tagged on the voter's list. It is my wish that the word *homemaker* will describe her more accurately, and that she will keep house rather than letting the house keep her from more important things. Some women would almost regret changing their cleaning day for their husband's funeral. I hope your wife will be a little more flexible than that. If you get a day off and feel like a change, I hope she will "take off" with you even if it means letting Susie wear her blouse for a second day.

Above all, I hope your wife isn't the nagging kind, but don't expect that she will never nag—they all do. A *chronic* nagger, however, is a real problem. No husband can please her. If you find your wife nagging all the time, try to discover the source of her discontent. She is either lacking fulfillment of her personal needs or is resentful over something she needs to bring out in the open. Open complaint is healthier than buried resentment. I hope after you clear up her problem that your wife will encourage you when you are discouraged, love you when you are upset, and scold you when you are wrong.

Perhaps you are surprised that I believe your wife should scold you. I have seen husbands whose wives always pat them on the back when sometimes they need to be faced honestly with kindly criticism. These men are living in a dream world, with the illusion that they make no mistakes, have no faults, and need no improvement. I hope your wife will tell you the "truth that hurts" when you need it and that you will not resent her criticism. Your mother can't criticize you anymore so perhaps you should listen to your wife.

That reminds me to say that I hope your wife will not expect you to be like her mother and her sisters. Many women feel that their husbands lack understanding, but when I inquire further I find that this criticism is often produced by an ignorance of the differences between the sexes. Sometimes you may not notice when your wife is on the point of tears and she will wonder why. A woman would discern this but you will be too preoccupied to see the symptoms. You will need to be told because you are a man. I hope your wife will understand this and not judge you to be heartless. If she is wise, she will eventually understand the differences between the male and female personality. Then she will not expect from you all the tenderness and understanding that only a woman, with her God-given equipment for motherhood, can provide.

Solomon, the wise man, said, "Whoso findeth a wife findeth a good thing."[1] Some days—dog days, when your whole domestic world falls in on you—you will feel like contradicting him. Take heart! Things will return to normal in a day or two. All husbands find that the wonderful girl they married is a bundle of contradictions at times. That is because she is a woman.

Wedding Wishes to the Bride

Perhaps June is about to burst into bloom and you will be one of its fairest flowers, or you may have chosen another time of year for your wedding. With stars in your eyes and hope in your heart, you will pledge your loyalty to the man with whom you expect to find understanding and security. I have a few wishes for you.

I hope the man you marry will have ambition and be a good provider, but I hope he's not a compulsive worker. I know women who would forego some of their luxuries to have more of their man. May you not find yourself tied to a human dynamo—a man who never takes time from his work to enjoy the little things that put the gravy into living. If you do, you will chafe under the pressure of being constantly organized. The atmosphere of your home will be like a factory at quitting time, and the tension will mount with the coming of children. Infantile dawdling is frustrating to such a high-geared husband. May your man have his ambition in just the right doses so that he will enjoy family life.

That, incidentally, is the most common complaint of wives— no companionship. A few, however, find their husbands the other extreme. I have observed the man who wants to fill his wife's whole world. The advent of a friend or relative whose company his wife enjoys is devastating to his ego. He wants *all* of her. This kind of male is usually thoughtful and generous, but his wife feels like a caged bird. A short session of freedom from her clinging mate will be a luxury. If this kind of husband would just drown his selfish fears long enough to open the cage door graciously, he would find his frustrated mate returning contentedly in a few hours. I hope your man will learn this lesson early in your marriage.

Perhaps you have fears of your husband being too domineering. I hope he won't be. I think, however, that you would be just as unhappy with a Mr. Milquetoast. It puts a strain on a wife when her man expects her to be the family "push." This kind of husband will lie in bed on Sunday morning while you rise and take the family to church. He may even declare in his most masculine tone that church is for women and children. He will bluster about how unruly Johnny is but will leave the discipline to you. If you buy a house, rent a trailer, plan a vacation, or purchase insurance, you will have to take the initiative. If the project succeeds, it will be his idea; if it does not, it will be explained as "your crazy brainstorm."

I hope your man will carry a good supply of tolerance. If not, he will spend his life heckling you and your children with comparisons. He will wonder why you can't cook like his mother and sew like his sister. Your children will not measure up to qualities he sees in various other children. He will make no allowance for personality differences. Whenever others do not agree with him they will be wrong. If every relationship does not fit his rigid pattern it will be abnormal. He will expect all women to have equal doses of femininity; all children to have equal amounts of submissiveness. He will be frustrated by the individuals who fail to fit his tailor-made concepts. You will have a long struggle to teach him tolerance, but it will be worth the effort. You will teach this lesson best by showing tolerance yourself.

You may not have this difficulty. You may have the other extreme—a husband who is so tolerant that he will accept anything, tolerating any situation without an effort to change it. I hope your man will have principles which he will refuse to surrender for anyone. When it comes to important issues, I hope he will take a firm stand. You will find such a husband a tower of strength to his family.

I imagine you are planning an attractive home. May your husband appreciate such a haven and the work you put into it. However, I hope he will realize that home is made up of atmosphere more than furniture. If he knows this he won't be running his fingers over table tops; he will be too busy appreciating the harmony which you have worked to create, despite a dozen juvenile disagreements. If your husband appreciates this side of your wifely duty, he won't complain if you have "cracked up" under one too many days of being a human bumper for everybody's clashes. He won't notice the dishes you left in the sink when you went visiting to regain your sanity. I hope he will listen sympathetically to your woes on such days, and accept your tears as a perfectly normal female safety valve.

I hope your husband will confide in you, too. It is frustrating to be the uninformed partner in a marriage. May you not have to wonder why your man came home from work "crabby," and not eventually be told. I hope he will talk out his problems and misunderstandings and not bury them in tense silence behind the sports page. If he begins this way, try to help him communicate, but don't snoop. Some women, you know, have the opposite problem. Their husbands are always moaning about something and never offer a strong crying shoulder to their wives.

Perhaps I've frightened you both with my hopes and fears. Never mind, no one has a mate without faults. When you see them, do not despair; there are thousands of other couples with the same problems. If you love your mate, you will find a solution—like the oyster! When it is annoyed by a grain of sand under its shell, it produces a pearl to smooth it over. Go ahead, marry your choice, and when you discover a grain of sand (and you will), go to work on it. Both your character and your mate's will be strengthened by the adjustments which the flaw will require of you.

In the next few chapters we explore some of the areas in which marital differences may develop, and some of the adjustments that others have made to these differences.

Part III

YOU AND YOUR MATE

9

Doesn't Marital Happiness Always Follow Love?

THE EARLY HEBREW SOCIETY encouraged young husbands to spend the first year of married life establishing their relationship with their wives. Mosaic law instructed, "When a man hath taken a new wife, he shall not go out to war, neither shall he be charged with any business: but he shall be free at home one year, and shall cheer up his wife he hath taken."[1]

Although this practice is impossible in our culture, it does make us consider the importance of early marital adjustment. Paul Landis in his book, *Making the Most of Marriage,* notes that marital adjustment is more successful if made early in the marriage.[2] This is perhaps because eagerness to succeed is greater during the first year, and because there is no previously fixed pattern of marital adjustment to be unlearned.

Every marriage needs some similarities in the mates but there will also be marked differences. The success of the union is not as much determined by the similarities as by the way the mates adjust to their differences.

To begin with, there are distinct basic differences between the male and female personalities. Some sociologists claim that these differences are merely the result of social conditioning. But the Bible reports that God created us male and female, and I do not believe this refers only to our physical makeup.[3] Does it seem sensible to believe that the God who made certain different colors to complement each other, and certain different sounds to harmonize with each other, would not create male and female personalities which complement each other and yet together produce a harmonious relationship?

Today some are even promoting the idea that two males or two females can live together successfully in a pseudo-marital relationship. All of these homosexual relationships are filled with conflict because they lack the male-female differences which create distance between the partners, allowing them individual movement and development. Added to male-female differences is the diversity in individual personalities built in by heredity and childhood environment. These two kinds of differences usually cause some conflicts in a marriage until mates learn to adjust to them. Adjustments will be necessary in many areas of their lives together. The real test of love is our willingness to accept and adjust to differences.

The nature of marital adjustment will be illustrated by case studies in the chapters which follow. These are not real examples but fictitious composites of many cases encountered during my years of counseling. If you find yourself in one of these examples, be assured that it is only because your situation is repeated in many other lives.

10

What Sexual Adjustment Will Be Necessary?

THE FIRST GENERAL AREA of differences between mates is in personal matters involving only the partners. Sex is one of these areas. Besides the usual male-female sexual differences, there are differences related to background and personality. The following cases illustrate some of the problems brought to counselors:

SANDRA AND WAYNE

Sandra, a bride of five months, confided that either she was sexually inadequate or her husband Wayne was oversexed. She was not sure which. Considerable discussion had taken place between them over this point, with Sandra accusing Wayne of being obsessed with sex, and he calling her frigid. Both became subjective and emotional. At times each produced guilt and self-consciousness in the other, and both regretted that they were not satisfying each other fully. Sandra sometimes feared that she was only wanted for sexual satisfaction; her husband feared that he was not loved because Sandra was not always eager for his sexual advances. Concerned and upset, Sandra sought outside help for she loved her husband and could not understand what was happening to their relationship.

It was reassuring to Sandra to discover that desire for intercourse usually occurs more frequently in the male than in the female. The subjective emotions that had gathered around their differences were removed when both mates understood these general male-female differences. Then they were free to accept each other and work objectively toward a satisfactory adjustment.

Lois and Jim

Lois, a sensitive idealistic girl of twenty-three, tearfully confessed to me that her husband Jim was indifferent to her feelings. "I always thought Jim was a considerate person before we married," she wailed, "but now he is harsh and thoughtless."

Her story revealed that one evening the couple had a minor disagreement. Jim was momentarily irritated and spoke sharply to her. Lois, having high expectations of marital bliss, was quite upset by the incident. Jim, being more realistic, dismissed the whole affair as a minor matter. Later that evening he was eager to make love to his wife, but his advances seemed to Lois to contradict his earlier words. Unable to respond in the least, she became upset over what she interpreted as his insincerity and recoiled at his advances. Now she pictured him as a feelingless creature who wished to carry out intercourse completely apart from feelings of love—a possibility that filled Lois with insecurity and forebodings. The next day her concern made her irritable and distant. However, her husband again tried to interest her in sexual intercourse the next night. Lois was perplexed and incensed and sought help.

It was surprising to Lois to discover that sexual desire in males is not as dependent on psychological closeness as in females. She learned that while a woman finds it difficult or impossible to respond sexually after a misunderstanding, a man will often desire intercourse at such times as reassurance that he is still loved in spite of the disagreement.

When this matter was clarified, Lois understood how each of their actions had upset the other—her husband feeling unloved because his wife failed to respond sexually, and she feeling unloved because her husband expected her to respond after a misunderstanding. When the mates accepted their differing male-female viewpoints, their tensions surrounding sexual matters diminished.

NORMA AND BOB

Norma, a shy woman of thirty who lacked self-confidence, came to discuss a problem. After talking about minor matters for some time, she finally ventured to inquire where she could get help with a sexual problem. When she was encouraged to confide, she stated that she was frigid. Further inquiry revealed that she sometimes desired sexual intercourse but was not always able to reach a climax.

"Bob and I read several books on the subject," she stated nervously, "and they seemed to teach clearly that both mates should always be fully satisfied. My husband always reaches a climax and I don't. I must be the one with the sex problem. One book especially made me feel that I need a psychiatrist to cure my frigidity."

After some discussion, Norma was reassured that she was not frigid. Frigidity involves an aversion to the sex act, which she did not feel. She also learned that her husband's sexual climax was so premature that he was contributing much to her problem. It was pointed out to her that couples often take time to adjust sexually and that, while simultaneous orgasm is the ideal in sexual adjustment, many couples do not reach the ideal all the time. Others take several months after they marry to learn to reach simultaneous orgasm. She was encouraged to take a more relaxed view of the problem so that overconcern would not create tension and make a successful climax more difficult. She agreed to go with her husband to their family doctor to talk over their problems if the situation failed to improve. Some helpful books were suggested to help them learn more about satisfying intercourse.[1]

When Norma and Bob learned that satisfactory sexual adjustment is a skill which takes time to learn, they realized that they were expecting too much in too short a time, especially when they had entered marriage with little knowledge of the techniques of sexual stimulation and intercourse. With help from the suggested reading and a talk with their family doctor, their adjustment improved greatly. Their concern over reaching simultaneous orgasm lessened and they were able to relax and enjoy the measure of adjustment which they had while working toward greater skill.

LUCY AND FRED

Lucy was reluctant and embarrassed when she mentioned her problem of sexual adjustment. She remarked that she never felt free to discuss sex at home and only came to me because she had no one else and she was greatly concerned. Finally she found words to express guilt over the mutual enjoyment she and her husband, Fred, found in many intimate caresses which preceded their intercourse. Although she had not expressed her guilt to Fred, she always felt depressed and unclean the next day. She wondered how she could help him see that their behavior was wrong.

Lucy was relieved when she discovered that sex play is an important prelude to intercourse and that she should feel no guilt about enjoying it. Any act preceding intercourse which is *pleasurable to both partners* and not physically injurious is acceptable. She learned that physical love should involve giving one's whole body to the loving caresses of one's mate. She was encouraged to read the love scenes of the Song of Solomon for help in understanding the erotic appeal of various parts of the body.

There are many variations of these sexual problems. Many sex differences may also result from one mate's unhealthy attitudes about the sex act. Some people have received the kind of sex education that has caused them to look upon sex as vulgar, animalistic or embarrassing. These learned attitudes will only be overcome by time and the patient understanding of the healthy mate. Some women consider sex as a male pleasure to be submitted to by women as a marital duty. If such unhealthy attitudes persist they will damage the sexual relationship and may need to be changed by professional help. However, love, patience and unselfishness will overcome most sexual difficulties.

A wise mate will neither exploit his partner nor continue to deny sexual satisfaction. The Bible teaches this clearly:

> The husband should give to his wife her conjugal rights . . . and likewise the wife to the husband. The wife does not have [exclusive] authority and control over her own body, but the husband [has his rights]; likewise also the husband does not have [exclusive] authority and control over his body, but the wife [has her rights]. Do not refuse and deprive and defraud each other (of your due marital rights), except by mutual consent for a time, that you may devote yourselves unhindered to prayer. But afterwards resume marital relations, lest Satan tempt you [to sin] through your lack of restaint of sexual desire.[2]

11

What Other Personal Differences Will We Discover?

THERE IS NO END to the number of major and minor personal differences that can arise to disturb a marital relationship—differences in eating habits and tastes, in preferences regarding room temperature, in sleep habits and a thousand other matters. But three common areas of personal difference require special attention: differences in pace, role interpretation, and the use of leisure time.

PACE

Differences in pace can cause discomfort in a marriage. I recall in my own marriage how this problem became distressing at times.

Vincent (HARE) Trimmer married Ellen (TORTOISE) McKay on July 6, 1940. For the first few years both of us felt frustrated by the other's pace. My husband jumps out of bed at dawn, usually before the alarm rings. He is running almost before his feet touch the floor. I sleep on, while the alarm runs down at my head and my husband gets breakfast.

When we walk together, I have trouble keeping up. When we read together, I finish every page long after he is ready to turn it. When we make a decision, I am still contemplating it long after my husband has decided. During the first three years of marriage, each of us tried to change the other's pace. Then, the wise old doctor who delivered our children took my husband aside and said, "Look! Your wife can't travel at your fast pace; it's not good for her health to be hurried all the time." She also helped me to realize that, because my man was very active and unusually quick, I must be willing to let him indulge in more activities than I am capable of handling.

Every individual has his pace and to change this defeats his efficiency and makes him feel either rushed or frustrated. There is no right pace or wrong pace, only a pace that is right for me and one that is right for you. Slow people sometimes accomplish as much as fast people, but to watch them do it is maddening to a highly geared individual. A slow person finds it hard to relax in the presence of a person of ceaseless activity. Acceptance of each other's differences in this matter is the only solution to the problem.

ROLE INTERPRETATION

Perhaps you are surprised that my husband makes breakfast. Don't be alarmed, his domestic duties end there. Often, if he wants a glass of milk, I pour it, because he claims it tastes better. His only effort at cooking a meal, soon after we were married, ended with the purchase of the ingredients. He came home with a cabbage and thought he had a head of lettuce and with four pounds of lamb chops when he was instructed to get four lamb chops. But tell me, which are male responsibilities in a marriage and which are female? Differing opinions on this question can cause tension.

Who should do the budgeting? Who should clean the cellar? Should the wife always get up at night with the baby? Who is responsible for the lawns, the shopping, taking junior to his music lesson, seeing junior's principal when he has problems at school?

In other cultures male and female roles are clearly defined. Certain responsibilities are always left to the husband; others are always given to the wife. Little conflict occurs in these cultures over role interpretation. In our culture, male and female responsibilities differ from home to home.

GEORGE AND JEAN

George came with just such a problem. He described his mother as a hard-working, responsible woman.

"I have no sisters," George explained, "so my mother was the only woman in our home. She was proud of her four sons, and gave her whole time to caring for us. She had no other interests.

"Last June I married Jean, a fine girl, who seemed responsible and efficient," he said. "I thought she would be like my mother —dedicated to her home and family. Now I find she loads half of her work on me."

"In what way?" I asked.

"Well, apparently Jean's father spoiled his wife—waited on her hand and foot," he said. "I don't want to spoil my wife; but when I put my foot down, she accuses me of being unreasonable and demanding."

"Give me specific instances," I said.

"Last week, on my way home from work, I bought some petunia plants. I thought Jean would appreciate having them for the front flower beds. When I showed them to her she seemed pleased, so I left them in the garage, expecting her to plant them the next day while I was at work. When I came home the next night they were not planted. I hated to make a fuss then because she had a fine dinner ready. Later I tackled the problem and asked why she didn't plant the petunias. She seemed hurt and said that she considered it a man's job. Her father always did the gardening, she explained. To keep peace, I planted the petunias while she washed the dinner dishes."

"Is that all?" I inquired.

"No," he replied, "the next day she forgot to remind me about my dental appointment and I missed it. I told her I had the appointment two weeks before—but did she remind me? Not on your life! I asked her why she failed to remind me like my mother always had and she blew up. She asked coldly if I thought everything was her responsibility and asked when I was going to clean the cellar. That did it! I told her that the house was her job—the garden and the cellar included. My job was earning a living. At that she burst into tears and sobbed something about wishing she had found a thoughtful man like her father. I felt guilty and sorry that I could not make her happy. I love my wife. How can I help learn to take responsibility?"

George resisted the idea that perhaps his mother had overplayed the female role. It was pointed out to him that he and Jean had differing ideas about the responsibilities of husbands and wives. Each agreed to stop insisting that the role interpretation of their parents be accepted as infallible and to begin working out a pattern acceptable to both of them. George finally admitted that keeping his appointments was in no way Jean's responsibility, and Jean decided that she didn't really mind working in the garden if George would work with her. Each mate accepted the other's viewpoint with less emotional heat and became objective enough to work out compromises.

LEISURE

I heard a young woman say recently that she and her husband have more disagreements during vacations than at any other time. Their ideas of leisure differ greatly and each wants the other to enjoy leisure in his way.

KAREN AND JOEL

Karen resented Joel's love of golf. She disliked sports, preferring to paint or listen to music. She enjoyed visiting friends, too, while Joel claimed that because he sees people all day, he wants to escape to the solitude of the golf course on days off.

"The only difference between weekends and weekdays," Karen said bitterly, "is that on weekends it's golf that takes Joel away, on weekdays it's work. I never get a chance to go on a painting trip because he has the car.

"We had a quarrel last night over our vacation plans. Joel wants to stay at a motel near a golf course where there is a good "pro." That means that I will sit alone most of the day while he golfs."

"What would you like to do for a vacation, Karen?" I asked.

"I wouldn't care as long as I could be with people. I'm tired of the isolation of our country home which Joel bought because he likes solitude."

"So both your needs must be met, Karen, in one vacation. Any suggestions how?" I ventured.

"Why can't he give up his golf?" Karen squirmed.

"For the same reason you can't give up people and your interests," I defended. "He needs it. When your differences are accepted by both of you, then you will find a plan which meets both your needs. How about a lodge with a golf course on the grounds or nearby? Must you insist that Joel give up his golf to enjoy people with you? He won't really enjoy them, you know."

"Silly isn't it?" Karen laughed. "I've been trying to make Joel enjoy my kind of vacation for years, spoiling both of our holidays with unpleasantness."

The next summer Karen and Joel went to a lodge with a golf course nearby. The lodge also held craft classes and Karen took painting lessons each morning while Joel golfed. Afternoons and evenings they spent together swimming and taking part in group activities. They made many new friends and came home contented because they both had a satisfying vacation. Some mates have solved the problem by taking part of their vacation separately with friends or relatives and part of it together.

Basic personal differences like these can eventually be accepted with good humor and tolerance. When this happens the very differences which could have been sources of conflict become evidences of love because they are recognized and accepted by each mate. As Paul admonished the Christians at Ephesus, "Accept life with humility and patience, making allowances for one another because you love one another,"[1] and again, "Husbands, love your wives—be affectionate and sympathetic with them—and do not be harsh or bitter or resentful toward them."[2]

12

What About Differences in Values?

EVERY INDIVIDUAL has a set of values which largely determine his choices. Economic values determine our attitudes to money, possessions and work; aesthetic values determine the kind of surroundings we choose; religious values affect our moral choices; and social values establish our relationship patterns.

When we marry, it is wise to choose a mate whose values are similar to our own, which usually happens if the two mates are from similar family backgrounds. However, there is always some diversity in values. One mate may set high priority on success while the other places importance on the social satisfactions of rich family life. One may highly value economic security while the other places priority on aesthetic fulfillment. In general, men place more priority on economic values and success than on social satisfactions, perhaps because they are the breadwinners. This conflict was evident in the case of Agnes and Peter.

WORK

AGNES AND PETER

Agnes and Pete were under pressure soon after their marriage because of Pete's dedication to his work. After three years of marriage Agnes felt lonely and frustrated because Pete gave his whole life to his position as a junior executive in an aircraft company.

"When Pete is home there's nothing left of him," Agnes complained. "He is often out of town all week and then comes home with an attaché case full of weekend work. This, he claims, is necessary to success. He keeps promising that things

will be better later. Marriage is a farce under these conditions,"
she fumed, "the only conversation I ever hear is baby talk. Last
night we had a blowup because Pete's company wants him to
attend a course every Saturday this winter. Where does a family
fit into this schedule?"

"This is unfortunate," I said. "And there are hundreds of
other homes facing the same problem. In our society a man's
importance seems to be measured by the shortness of his visits
home. We are technologically knowledgeable and socially in-
competent in our society, but this is life for today's executive.

"Tell me, Agnes, even though the quantity of time you spend
with Pete is limited, what about the quality of your relationship
when he is home? What happens when you are together?"

Agnes looked at the floor and her face flushed. "Nothing
special," she said, avoiding my gaze.

"You must really appreciate each other's company when you
are together so little," I said, hoping she would be honest with
me.

Tears spurted from her eyes and Agnes shook with sobs. "I
hate what happens when Pete comes home," she wailed, "but
I can't help it. It's not fair! Not a bit fair!"

"What happens, Agnes?" I said quietly. "This is Friday. I
suppose Pete will be home tomorrow. Now tell me what will
happen."

"But you'll think I'm a miserable shrew if I tell you," she
defended.

"Do you want help or don't you, Agnes?"

"Well, when he comes through the door with that detestable
attaché case, I'll give him a wifely peck and say, 'Get washed.
Your dinner has been getting cold for fifteen minutes.' He'll
notice the big scab on Joey's knee and ask about it. 'He's been
a bad boy all week,' I'll tell him. 'He wouldn't walk like I told
him when we went to the store Monday but ran ahead of me
and fell. Besides that, the switch on my washer went on the
blink and I didn't get any washing done till the repair man
came on Wednesday. That's not all. I couldn't go to the

shower I was looking forward to Thursday because the baby-sitter was sick. I wish I had a husband to baby-sit and do all the things I suppose a proper husband does around a house.' "

"Then what?" I urged.

"Then Pete will sigh, look angry, loosen his tie, and head for the washroom, closing the door firmly after him."

"Then?"

"Then I will holler, 'Are you coming, Pete? This food is getting as cold as a stone. I thought you might take me somewhere tonight but the evening is half over now.' Then Pete will come to the table and slump into his chair.

" 'I'm too tired to go out; I've had a hard week,' he will say, and later withdraw into dismal silence behind the newspaper."

"Do you need to go any further, Agnes, or do you see your contribution to the problem?"

"No wonder I'm miserable!" she defended.

"But are you making the best of a bad situation? You know, happy mates make happy marriages. Are you happy?"

"How can I be?"

"Is happiness on the outside or on the inside? Paul said, 'I have learned, in whatsoever state I am, therewith to be content.'[1] When he wrote these words he was being unjustly held in prison—not really a fair situation. Do you think you could learn this?"

"I sure need to," she said.

"From Pete's point of view, you are making it hard for him. The book of Proverbs describes a contentious wife as being like 'a continual dropping in a very rainy day.'[2] 'It is better to dwell in the wilderness,' it says, 'than with a contentious and an angry woman.'[3] It's a habit, Agnes, that grows from resentment and discontent. Perhaps if you lick this problem, your whole situation will improve. With your support Pete could reach his goal sooner and have more time for his home. While we don't approve of the business practices which make Pete's life the way it is, we can't always change them."

In four weeks Agnes came back.

"You wouldn't believe the change," she said. "After I talked with you I read a prayer in the newspaper—'God give me the serenity to accept the things I cannot change, the courage to change the things I can, and the wisdom to know the difference.'

"Now the times that Pete and I spend together are great. Lately he has been pushing himself a bit harder during the week. He gets home earlier and with less weekend work. I'm beginning to think some of his dedication to his work was to escape from his contentious wife," she laughed. "Pete and I are much happier since I accepted the situation, and Joey is a much more contented little boy.

"And guess what! I'm taking a correspondence course in journalism. I've always wanted to write, and now I hope to learn. Pete thinks my first lesson shows real talent. We're both happy over it. It's great to be out of that old complaining habit, but it sure is easy to get back into it."

This is a common pressure placed on young marriages by our competitive society. However, some mates have risen above these difficulties and built a happy marriage.

Money

The word *extravagance* brings different mental concepts to different people. What meets my needs is not an extravagance to me, and what meets your needs is not an extravagance to you. But what seems necessary to me may appear extravagant to you.

A wife may say to her husband, "Why pay all that money to attend a football game when you can see it on television?" He knows he can't feel the same about it on television. A husband may ask, "Why do you need a new dress when the one you have looks lovely on you?" To her, a new dress gives confidence and a feeling of well-being.

Differences in the values of people are revealed in their use of money. Norman valued saving more than spending, while his wife valued spending as a symbol of being loved.

JENNIFER AND NORMAN

Norman, a reserved young accountant who exuded carefulness, came to discuss what he referred to as a minor problem. His wife, Jennifer, an outgoing vivacious girl of twenty-five, had been married to him for about one year. Norman got right to the point and admitted rather sheepishly that, the night before, his wife had called him stingy and accused him of not loving her.

With further inquiry he revealed that Jennifer had bought a hat which cost her $15.00 when, he said, she already had more hats than the closet shelf could hold. When Norman asked her why she bought it, she said, "Because I felt like something new and you never buy me a thing." He explained to her that she would have to curb her buying because she had already exceeded her clothes budget and was using money he intended to save for the new car which they both wanted. He also pointed out to her that good financing requires the saving of 5 percent of one's income, and her spending had made this impossible.

Jennifer blew up. "You don't love me!" she told him. "You never bring home surprises like my father brought my mother —flowers, perfume, candy. . . . You are more interested in hoarding your money in the bank."

"I was very surprised," Norman said, "at Jenny's attitude. As if buying things could be a proof of love. My father never bought things like that for my mother, but he saved carefully and invested in mortgages. Now he collects payments from fifteen mortgages and has increased his income so much that he recently bought a beautiful new home. I thought saving for future security was a proof of my love for my wife, but I guess she has other ideas."

Norman was helped to see that he and Jennifer, because of their family backgrounds, had very different ideas about money. Jennifer saw spending as an expression of love; Norman saw saving as an expression of love. His attempts to save for his wife's security were being interpreted as a lack of love.

Money means different things to different people. To an in-

tellectual, money means books; to his wife, it may mean beauty;
to an aesthetic person, it represents cultural satisfactions; to a
sportsman, it means recreation.

As time passes, each mate will learn what the other's peculiar
needs are, and together they will plan their budget to meet both
their needs.

BRENDA AND STEVE

Brenda and Steve had been married one year. Both were
employed and were hoping someday to save the down payment
for a house. But recently they had been quarreling because of
financial pressures. Finally they came for help with the conflict
that was upsetting their marriage.

Brenda, age twenty-six, was depressed and discouraged.

"Steve has bought so many things on credit that by the time
we meet the monthly payments there is nothing left for sav-
ings," she confided. "We have large accounts at three department stores, and we owe two loans to finance companies. When
we need clothes, we have to charge them because we have no
free money. Now Steve wants to get another finance company loan to pay two gasoline accounts which are in arrears
because he used the money for a new stereo. I keep telling him
we're getting in deeper all the time, but he only thinks about
getting immediate cash. He never considers the cost of loans."

Steve sheepishly mumbled something about his wife being
a pessimist. "All young couples are in debt," he argued. "If
we can get a loan, we can tide ourselves over the tough time
and get on our feet. Women don't know anything about
finances anyway."

Half an hour later, pencil and paper had proved to Steve
that he was dead wrong. We started with the revolving credit
accounts and computed how much the use of someone else's
money was costing him at 24 percent annual interest. His used
car, we found, had been purchased at an easy-credit car lot at 30
percent interest per year. Now he was about to enter into another loan at 24 percent interest. Of course these interest rates

had been quoted on a monthly basis and he did not realize what the annual percentage would be. Careful accounting revealed that the couple would be paying $1,000.00 interest in the next year on debts amounting to just over $5,000.00. If they were late with payments it might be more. Steve was horrified at this discovery.

"What can we do?" he asked helplessly.

"Well, certainly not run up more debts," Brenda snapped.

"One thing is sure," I commented. "You'll have to stop blaming each other."

Brenda and Steve wrote their creditors, asking for more time. Some firms were even willing to stop interest during the waiting period. Both mates agreed not to use credit until their bills were paid. They drew up a budget which allowed for necessities and gradually they lowered their debts.

"It's a lot easier to get into debt than to get out of it," Brenda observed on their last visit.

"The funny part of it is," Steve added, "when you plan your spending instead of just making snap decisions, you seem to be able to have more of the things you want."

"That's right," Brenda said, "and less quarreling over them."

Brenda and Steve experienced a problem which is one of the chief sources of marital discord. I thought how much more serious their financial condition might have been if Brenda had not come for help and thus stopped Steve's reckless spending. They would have become acquainted with garnishees, court judgments and bailiffs, and their marital conflict would have been even greater.

RELIGION

The effects of mixed religion and of irreligion on a marriage have been discussed in the chapter "How Will I Know When I Find the Right Mate?" Differences in religious values and beliefs can put considerable strain on a marriage, especially when each mate insists on the children being taught in his or her religion. If a couple shares vital Christian faith in God then they have a strength in their union which can be found in nothing else. As the Kinsey Report admits, religious faith is the greatest deterrent to marital infidelity.

These are just a few examples of the most common sources of marital conflict over values. No wonder God instructed husbands to love their wives as their own selves,[4] and wives to adapt themselves to their own husbands.[5] That means that both husband and wife will plan for the comfort, convenience and happiness of the other. With this attitude, adjustment in all of these areas will be possible.

13

Are In-laws Really Such a Problem?

WE DEALT in the last few chapters with tensions resulting from basic personal differences. There are also marital stresses caused by other relationships. Marriage partners cannot "live unto themselves," and each has other attachments which sometimes complicate marital adjustment.

IN-LAWS

Adjustment to personal differences is sometimes hindered by in-law interference. Each individual learns a certain pattern of homelife from his childhood environment, and when there is no interference from the two sets of parents, the differing patterns of the young mates are changed and integrated until their marriage has formed its own concept of homelife. This pattern is neither that of the wife's background nor that of the husband's early environment but one which may include elements of both. These elements of their relationship are mutually chosen and tested by the young couple to meet their own needs. While this adjustment is being made, and the new pattern emerging (hopefully early after marriage) it is frustrating and damaging to the newlyweds to have either of their parents trying to impose their ways on the young couple. Although such interference may be well intended, it hinders marital adjustment. The problem is not geographical but psychological. Parents living under the same roof may interfere less than those living half a continent away. Emotional involvement, not physical proximity, does the damage. A young wife feels guilty about giving her first loyalty to her husband because of unhealthy emotional ties with her father. A young husband feels disloyal if he goes against the advice of his overprotective mother. This is why Scripture states three times that when a man marries, he should "leave his father and his mother, and shall cleave unto his wife."[1]

JOAN AND CHARLES

Joan was thirty when she married Charles. They had been engaged three years before she could be persuaded to leave her family, a closely knit little group where even the grown children were included in the parent's social life. Charles respected his in-laws but had hoped that once Joan was in her own home she would loosen her family ties. Before long he realized that he was having in-law trouble and requested help.

"How do you wean a thirty-year-old from her parents and the rest of the brood?" he asked.

"What makes you think she isn't weaned?" I inquired.

"In the last week we haven't had dinner alone once. First Joan's mother had picked a batch of green peas and we just had to help eat them. The next night Joan's kid brother arrived with strawberries and Joan invited him to eat with us. The next day she went home to use her mother's sewing machine and left me a note, 'Come over to Mother's for dinner.' Yesterday was my wife's bowling day. Since her mother bowls on the same team, she brought Mom home for supper. When my wife said we were invited to her parent's cottage for the weekend, I put my foot down. 'Do you think I married your whole family?' I asked.

"She began to cry and said that I was cruel to try to isolate her from her family when they meant so much to her. She said it was too bad that I didn't appreciate them after they had been so kind to me. I told her their kindness made me feel like a mouse in a trap. Am I wrong to want my wife to myself," he asked, "or should I share her with them every day in the week?"

"Did you discuss this obvious problem before you married her?" I inquired.

Charles admitted that he had avoided discussing her relationship with her family before marriage because he thought if he pushed her she might choose her family rather than him.

"Joan will need some time and patient handling before she will be able to loosen her family ties," I observed. Fortunately Joan loved Charles deeply and was quite distressed to see his unhappiness over their lack of privacy. Later she was able to see that her first loyalty now belonged to Charles and that she should be the one to discourage her family from so many contacts and involvements with her. Charles, on the other hand, accepted the fact that he had married into a close family and that perhaps because he had loosened his family ties at a young age when he joined the air force, he did not quite appreciate the difficulty involved in Joan's adjustment in this matter.

They agreed on a weekly visit from or to Joan's family. Then they worked together in developing friendships with other couples. Joan gradually began to confide more in a close friend than in members of her family. This minimized her family's involvement in the marriage. Gradually she was able to wean herself from dependence on her family and to teach them respect for the privacy of her new home.

Such a happy solution is not always found. Studies by Paul H. Landis indicate that of all married couples studied, one in ten have failed to solve their in-law problems after more than twenty years of marriage.[2] Evelyn Duvall, notes in her book *In Laws: Pro and Con* that a Cornell University research team ranks in-law trouble as the third most common cause of marital disagreement and as the first cause of marital breakdown during the first year of marriage.[3] The interfering mother-in-law with her meddlesome-possessive-nagging syndrome is the most disturbing in-law. Folklore points to the *wife's* mother as the prime offender, but recent writings single out the *husband's* mother as the chief source of interference.

GRACE AND WILF

Grace and Wilf struggled with this problem. Long after their fifteenth anniversary, Grace had not gained a wife's place in the interest and affections of her husband. He spent many of his evenings and much of his money on his elderly mother even though she had several other children to care for her.

"Our family just doesn't count because his mother comes first," Grace confided. "We get whatever is left of his time, interest and money. His mother is a demanding person who keeps him busy most of the time. Painting, gardening and repairs are taken care of at her home while ours is neglected. If we are invited to a social event, Wilf usually refuses because he is busy with his mother. Our children really have no father because he is too busy being a model son."

Wilfred rejected all attempts to show him his responsibility to Grace and their family. Eventually she resigned herself to a hopeless situation—at least until his mother dies.

JUDY AND HAROLD

Another young woman, Judy, confided that her mother-in-law had ruined her marriage.

"My husband, Harold, consults his mother before every decision he makes," Judy said. "Even if I disagree with his mother, he goes ahead in favor of her advice. She is always loaning him money but constantly criticizes him for being useless and dependent. When this happens Harold gets upset and takes his bad mood out on me because he is afraid to tell his mother off. There is no partnership in our marriage because Harold has never gone out of partnership with his mother. I feel like an intruder in their relationship."

Harold refused to admit to any problem in the marriage and, as long as I had contact with the family, the mother continued to call all the moves. The son, an inadequate, dependent, but very hostile individual, was paying homage at his maternal shrine. Although deep in his personality he resented her control, he did not have the strength to break away from it.

Fortunately these are the unhappy exceptions. Many young people enjoy meaningful relationships with both sets of parents while maintaining their own autonomy as mature adults. The parents neither expect nor receive their first loyalty.

14

Will Children Cement Our Marriage?

HOW MANY TIMES well-meaning advice-givers have glibly predicted that all of the conflicts in an upset marriage would disappear with the coming of children. Sometimes this happens, but often a hitherto peaceful relationship will experience new and unexpected tensions with the arrival of a child. Sometimes tension increases as the family grows older.

COMPETITION

Parenthood may promote maturity in a young couple, but conversely, this new responsibility can overwhelm an immature mate. For example, a sense of competition may develop in an immature husband when the new baby arrives. This situation surprised both Joyce and Milton.

JOYCE AND MILTON

Joyce, an eighteen-year-old, was thrilled when her first child was placed in her arms by a nurse. She reveled in watching his daily development and enjoyed his dependence upon her. Whenever Milton, age nineteen, visited, his wife talked of nothing but the new baby. He brought her roses and chocolates and tried to tell her how lonely it was at home without her, but her response was disappointing to him. Her whole interest seemed transferred to this new little intruder.

When Joyce arrived home, her whole world seemed to be filled with diapers and bottles. Milton felt like an outsider in his own home. Resentment and jealousy rose in his heart, for which he hated himself. "Fathers are proud of their sons, not jealous of them," he told himself, but he could not shake his unwelcome feelings. One day, when he felt a deep need for affection and appreciation, Joyce brushed him off with some comment about the diapers in the sink. Milton exploded and all his pent-up feelings poured out. Joyce responded with a sarcastic remark about his childishness and stomped off to wash the diapers. The next day she confided her anxiety to me.

She was reassured to find that young husbands often have quite an adjustment to make at the arrival of a child. An insecure man, she learned, may not be able to control his feelings at having to share his partner with his child, especially if his wife overplays her mother role to the exclusion of her role as a wife. Joyce admitted that she had become too preoccupied with motherhood and deserved part of the blame for Milton's behavior.

That evening she apologized to her husband for not understanding and appreciating his needs. The next evening the couple planned a brief outing between the baby's feedings. Seeing his wife dressed up and having her full attention did wonders for Milton. He gradually lost his jealous feelings and accepted Joyce's mother role. He helped her with some of the extra work so that she would not be overtired and even took care of the baby occasionally to give her a change. Within a few months, both mates had made a happy adjustment to having a baby in the home. Joyce returned to being an attentive wife, and Milton stopped being just a husband and became a proud father.

CHILD-RAISING

Another conflict which parenthood may bring to a marriage, especially as the children grow older, is conflict over methods of child-raising.

SUSAN AND JOHN

John's father, a European immigrant, saw child-raising as a purely authoritarian relationship. He felt that a parent's role was to command right behavior, and a child's response should be immediate and unquestioning obedience. His standards were lofty and his demands difficult. When his children failed to measure up, he made ample use of "the rod."

Susan's father, a rather quiet man, ruled his home with a less authoritarian approach. He laid down rules regarding important matters but in lesser matters gave his children considerable choice of action. Susan had grown up without much trouble because when she wanted to disobey her parents she could not carry it through because she loved and respected her father too much to hurt him by her disobedience.

When a son came into their home, Susan and John were thrilled. During the child's infancy everything went fairly well, but when he started school, tension grew between them because of John's authoritarian methods of discipline. John resented Susan's interference and her tendency to shield their son from his father's discipline. Susan was troubled by what she considered John's too-strict control. After an especially stormy session she came for counseling.

It was pointed out to her that their concepts of child-training, which they learned from their own parents, were different. Her husband's view of training a child was authoritarian, while her own concept placed more emphasis on self-expression and self-determination and was therefore more permissive. The motivation of each parent was love for the child and a desire to help him grow up successfully. In this, there was perfect harmony. Therefore they had to build on this point of agreement. If John found it impossible to modify his authoritarian methods after Susan explained her viewpoint, that was his privilege. Susan was helped to see that she could do great harm to her child by nullifying her husband's attempts to discipline him. Even though his methods were different from hers, she must remember that John, whom she greatly respected and admired, was raised by authoritarian methods and had matured into healthy manhood, just as she, raised by more permissive standards, had matured into healthy womanhood. The essential ingredients of effective discipline are mature love and concern for the welfare of the child. If these qualities are present, the methods can differ greatly from home to home and the end results can still be successful.

After our talk, Susan attempted to stop interfering with her husband's discipline, even though his methods still seemed strict by her standards. Later she confided that after she stopped trying to force John to adopt her more permissive methods, he softened his discipline considerably. He told her later that while she kept "riding" him about his strictness, he felt the need to be even more strict to balance what he viewed as her too permissive attitudes. Now that she no longer sheilds the boy, his father is less strict.

DOROTHY AND ALEX

Dorothy had the opposite problem. She stormed into the office, her square jaw set with determination. She explained that, while her husband, Alex, was a kindly, lovable person, he was a "washout" as a father. She told how, in her childhood home, her father, a decisive, fast-thinking person like herself, had controlled his large family with orderly commands and strict discipline. He seemed always to sense trouble before it happened and kept a firm rein on his children.

"But Alex is no father at all," she charged. "He is a social worker in the local psychiatric clinic and he always claims we need to try to find out why our daughter is so hostile and aggressive. He claims my way of handling her is not helping, but what does he do? Nothing!

"Now, yesterday, for instance," she went on, "Alex and Lynne, our ten-year-old daughter, were in the living room while I prepared dinner in the kitchen. Lynne began bouncing her ball around the room. The last time she did that she broke a favorite vase of mine. Her father, who was buried in a book at the time, claims he was just about to do something about the situation when I stormed into the room and gave her a good swat across the side of the head and yelled, 'Put that ball away!'

Lynne was furious and yelled back at me, and when her father tried to quietly reason with her, I exploded.

" 'I always have to hand out all the discipline in this house,' I said, 'and you never notice what's going on until it's too late. Maybe you're a good social worker, but as a father you're a washout.' Then, after I saw how much I had upset Alex, I was sorry and wished I could control my temper better."

Dorothy was helped to see that perhaps the best thing that could happen to Lynne was to be left to her father's slow, quiet method of handling discipline. She admitted that she never had waited to see if he could handle Lynne but had always stepped in and taken over before he had a chance to act. So she tried leaving the initiative to Alex and found that his quiet firmness did wonders for their explosive child. Lynne became less hostile and provoking, and her mother was forced to reassess her ideas about discipline. Alex, feeling that he now had the responsibility of discipline, made himself more available and became alert to situations and less preoccupied with other things.

15

Will Relationships Outside the Family Cause Tension?

SOMETIMES a marriage partner sees his spouse's friends or acquaintances as a threat to their marriage. Often this anxiety is unfounded; sometimes it is justified. The following are examples of tensions caused by associations outside the family:

FRIENDS

Good friends are a blessing and are not ruled out by marriage. How often a man finds strength and courage in the counsel of a male friend, especially when he faces problems which his wife has never experienced. A woman likewise finds comfort in a female friend in matters which a man is incapable of understanding. Although most people need several close relationships to satisfy them, friends have been the source of marital tension.

MARIE AND BILL

Marie and Bill were the most popular young couple in their church—bubbling, outgoing Marie and stable, quiet Bill. People noticed that after their marriage Marie spearheaded their social relationships. She had been just what Bill needed to encourage him to become involved socially. It surprised the minister of her church when Marie requested counseling.

"Bill is a wonderful husband, Pastor," she said, "you know that. But we have one disagreement that has come up before in our marriage, and now it is bothering us again."

"That surprises me, Marie," the pastor said, "but really, it shouldn't, since no marriage is completely free of problems."

"Well, you see, Pastor, Bill doesn't seem to need any close friends. He seems fully satisfied with me, but I'm different. I need intimate friendships too. Bill can't understand this because he thinks that he should satisfy all my social needs. We have had some rather strained discussions over this matter, especially when I have planned an evening with a friend. He says he's not jealous, but when I come home he seems quiet and almost sulky."

The minister nodded and Marie continued.

"Well, Pastor, the whole thing came to a head recently when Charlotte started coming to church. You know Charlotte, she's a divorcee and I feel sorry for her because she is always alone.

"I suggested to Bill that we drive her to church, and because we come together she sits with us. Recently she began dropping in at the house a couple of times a week. I really enjoy Charlotte's company. I haven't been going out at all without Bill because it seemed to cause a little friction. When Charlotte started dropping in, I encouraged it because it seemed to fill a need for me and also for Charlotte. Last night all three of us were invited over to the Browns for the evening with other church people. When I told Bill that I promised to pick Charlotte up and take her with us, he looked angry and said 'You pick her up. I don't feel like going anyway.'

"I was shocked and urged him to go. I commented that before our marriage he never attended parties and I hoped he wasn't falling into his old rut. When he mumbled something about not being interested in a threesome, I knew what was upsetting him. Now," Marie said, "I'm in the unhappy situation of having to hurt either Bill or Charlotte to solve the problem."

After much discussion, Marie admitted that she had a greater than average need to be with people and that Bill was perhaps threatened by her other relationships. Her outgoing friendliness had captured his interest and filled his world. His love for her was intense and satisfying, but Marie, with her wide social needs, required friends as well as a husband. In trying to restrict her social contacts to please Bill, Marie had created a vacuum which Charlotte came to fill. She had gone overboard in her new friendship and Charlotte, perhaps because of her loneliness, had overresponded to Marie's care for her.

Marie caught the picture as she talked about it. She later told Bill that she had been selfish and inconsiderate in always having Charlotte with them. She encouraged others in the church to spend time with Charlotte. After explaining to Bill that she needed close female friendships, he admitted that he had been selfish in not letting her satisfy her social needs. He now occupies himself happily while Marie enjoys an occasional evening with a friend—sometimes Charlotte and sometimes others. Recently a new couple, Jill and Jerry, came to the church, and Bill and Marie often spend an evening with them. Bill is learning to widen his social circle to include friendship with Jerry, and Marie finds satisfaction in Jill's company.

WORK ASSOCIATES

JUNE AND ANDREW

June felt threatened by her husband's relationship with his receptionist. June is from a broken home; her father deserted her mother for another woman when she was ten. At thirteen her parents' marriage ended in divorce.

When June met Andrew, an intern at the hospital where she trained, she was sure it was the most wonderful thing that had ever happened to her. In two years they married and Andrew began his medical practice. At first he was not busy and, although they were living on a limited income, they were happy together. Then tension mounted as his practice grew. June became concerned and shared her problem with me.

"At first Andrew and I were so happy," she confided. "He was like oil on the waters of my anxiety-ridden nature. I felt secure for the first time since my father left home. Then Andrew's practice grew and he hired a receptionist. Every week since then he has spent more time at the office and less time at home. He seems preoccupied and a bit distant at times."

"Why did this happen?" I asked.

"What else could I believe but that the receptionist is the cause of the change? It seemed to happen about that time. She phones for Andrew in emergencies sometimes. She sounds lovely! She's single and Andrew says she is very efficient with his books and courteous with the patients. He seems very pleased with her. I know I shouldn't mistrust him, but I guess I'm suspicious of men."

"But mistrust can undermine your relationship. Do you have any reason to suspect him of being interested in his receptionist?"

"Just putting the pieces together," she said. "His preoccupation, his long absences, his talk about how pleased he is with the girl—it all adds up."

"For a girl whose father ran off with another woman, it does," I said.

"Do you really think I'm imagining?"

"You could be, June."

"How can I find out?"

"Drop in at his office some afternoon."

June phoned three days later. "Forget the problem," she said. "There is none."

"Good. How do you know?" I asked.

"I went to the office and found Andrew swamped with work."

" 'Could you give shots to some of these patients?' he said. 'Maybe then I could catch up with my appointments.'

"I helped him until he slumped exhausted into a chair in the empty waiting room.

" 'I'll just have to get a nurse, June, I can't handle it all anymore.'

" 'When do I start?' I said.

"Andrew was so pleased that he threw his arms around me. Just then the receptionist poked her head in the door to announce that she was going home. I looked at her amused face and thought what a fool I had been."

June is not alone with her problem. Many times marital

difficulty arises from fears planted years before by the traumatic experiences of childhood. When a mate expects his partner to cut off all other relationships, he is both selfish and unrealistic. It is important to develop trust so that other relationships will not disturb the marriage.

If another individual does alienate the affections of a marriage partner, it is often only a temporary and passing attraction. A wise and mature mate will remain loyal and seek to correct in his own relationship the dissatisfactions that may have caused his partner to wander temporarily. Even when the mate has committed adultery, this is not necessarily the end of the marriage. There have been cases where many happy years of marriage have followed when a mate has been willing to forgive a temporary period of unfaithfulness. A continuous pattern of unfaithfulness is a different matter, and under these conditions a mate is justified in seeking legal separation or divorce.

16

When Is a Marriage Counselor Necessary?

THE MARITAL TENSIONS discussed in the preceding chapters are sometimes found in healthy marriages. They can be overcome by the normal processes of marital adjustment as the relationship matures. Other marriages, however, have more serious problems, creating emotional dynamics destructive to the formation of a satisfactory relationship.

UNCONSCIOUS FORCES AFFECT MARRIAGES

Schopenhauer, in his fable of the porcupines, gives an illustration of this kind of relationship. He tells of two freezing porcupines who needed to be close for mutual warmth, but every time their need brought them together they were mutually irritated by each other. Their need drew them together but their quills forced them apart. Some marriages (as well as parent-child relationships) fit this picture.

In cases where there seem to be unconscious forces pushing a couple apart in spite of their conscious desire to be close to each other, there may be a need for professional help. These forces are often unconscious attempts to reproduce something out of one's past, to relive old relationships, to wipe out old hurts, and to settle old conflicts.

For example, a young man who has had an unsatisfactory early relationship with his mother, chooses a wife with whom he unconsciously expects to satisfy his unmet dependency needs. When his wife, not wishing to be his mother, fails to respond in a motherly way, he transfers all the dependency and hostili-

ty from his unsuccessful mothering experience to his wife. He
feels that she, like his mother, has rejected him. Neither of the
partners can understand the husband's attitudes and behavior
before going to a marriage counselor. There they become
aware that the real source of the husband's unfair and irrational
feelings and behavior is that he is repeating his early maternal
relationship in his marriage. Given this insight, the partners
are more tolerant of each other and can work together at break-
ing the vicious circle of destructive feelings that are pushing
them apart.

Many times these phantoms from the past—persons with
whom an individual has had disturbing relationships—will
haunt adult relationships. The drama of the past, with all its
accompanying negative emotions, will then be replayed on the
stage of the present. No wonder a marriage partner is puzzled
by the inappropriate and unfair responses of his mate who
claims to love.

Sometimes both mates, having meshing neuroses, will continue for years to act out the opposite roles in the drama of early
infancy. For this type of marital problem, normal methods of
discussion and adjustment have little effect because the cause of
the differences is not on a conscious level. It is wise then to
seek professional help before the relationship deteriorates into
a mutually destructive one.

The best place to look for help is at an agency such as the
Family Service Association. Sometimes family courts also provide marital counseling. If psychiatric help is required by one
or both mates a trained counselor will suggest referral. If there
is no such agency, mental health clinics are available at most
large hospitals. If it is possible to find a professional who shares
the couple's faith, this is fine; but, if not, other help must be
accepted. Most counselors will respect a person's genuine faith
in God even if they do not share it. Even if a counselor opposes
a client's beliefs, he will not succeed in disturbing them unless
the client's faith is a mere neurotic escape from guilt or a for-
malistic set of rules and regulations.

Several patterns are found in marriages where destructive unconscious forces are at work. The following are only a few.

THE AGGRESSIVE-SUBMISSIVE COMBINATION

The aggressive-submissive combination is found in the marriage where one mate is aggressive, unkind, humiliating and hurtful, while the other mate is usually dependent and submissive—a martyr filled with guilt and self-loathing who suffers sweetly, regardless of how he is treated. Usually the suffering partner invites ill-treatment because he has severe neurotic guilt from early childhood relationships, and these feelings are relieved by punishment. The destructive dynamics in this marriage indicate a need for professional counseling.

THE DETACHED-DEPENDENT COMBINATION

Another pattern is seen in the marriage where one mate is distant, rigid, ungiving, austere and detached. The other mate is a dependent, emotional person who has a craving for many spontaneous expressions of affection. The detached mate has been chosen because he seemed strong, thus able to meet the needs of his dependent partner. After marriage, what appeared to be strength in the detached mate turns out to be a defense, covering his fear of close emotional involvement. When the dependent mate seeks expressions of affection, the detached partner's defenses are threated and he withdraws, becoming even more detached. Thus each mate's reaction disturbs the other.

BATTLE-FOR-POWER COMBINATION

Other marriages are like a political power struggle, with each mate trying to dominate the other. Soon after marriage, both are on the defensive. Many violent quarrels may develop over decisions about purchases, discipline of their children, and a thousand other matters. Each partner is critical of the other, and takes every opportunity to humiliate his mate both privately and publicly. Often the children are involved in the power struggle. Eventually these partners tear each other down so constantly that each must find ego satisfaction outside of the home and apart from the mate. When the marital partner is not present to humiliate and criticize, his mate can find comfort for his battered ego. Thus, the partners gradually drift apart and satisfy their normal emotional needs in other people. Eventually the only satisfaction in the relationship is the power struggle satisfying each partner's neurotic need to dominate. Perhaps because of this, these marriages legally continue long after there is a breakdown on every level but the power struggle.

THE HELPER-HELPLESS COMBINATION

Another fairly common pattern is the helpless mate with the overly considerate partner. Each role is one side of the coin of dependency. One mate plays the part of the helpless infant, the other the part of the all-giving mother. The helpless person will find endless excuses for dependency, varying from illness to depression. This relationship usually ends in resentment when one mate fails to meet the excessive demands of the other. Once again, as in early childhood, the helpless mate is frustrated in his infantile longing for dependency. He feels guilty over his excessive demands, and anxious because they are not met.

MENDING A SICK MARRIAGE

These patterns are seldom found in neat categories, as this description may indicate, but are observed in endless variations resulting from the multitude of differing childhood conflicts which produce them.

If any of these patterns seem to be present to a disturbing degree in a marriage, it is wise to seek help—not the help of a willing neighbor or relative but the help of a trained social worker or psychiatrist. Procrastination only sacrifices the advantage of early diagnosis and treatment, thus causing greater damage to the children in the marriage.

Considerable public pessimism exists in regard to mending sick marriages. The neighbors may wonder why the mates don't separate and find another partner if they can't get along.

In the church, people are likely to tell them that if they were more spiritual the whole problem would solve itself. Certainly an intimate relationship with God improves one's social adjustment and gives courage and stamina to face experiences that bring self-awareness. However, there may be a need for professional diagnosis and treatment as well as for spiritual help.

Phillip Polatin and Ellen C. Philtine in their book *Marriage in the Modern World* state that "to allow a marriage to expire without benefit of any professional advice is like allowing a person to die without calling in a doctor."[1] They note that there is far too much pessimism abroad regarding the possibility of saving a marriage. In the book *With This Ring,* Louis Burke, a family court judge, has given case histories of seemingly hopeless marital situations and tells how they were saved by counseling.[2] In some cases the mates had even resorted to physical violence.

ALCOHOLISM AND MARRIAGE

Sometimes a destructive pattern in a marriage will be further complicated by the compulsive use of alcohol. Everyone is familiar with the home where one parent is an alcoholic. In the United States, 50 percent of all first admissions to mental hospitals suffer from alcoholism. It is also estimated that 30 to 40 percent of all delinquent youths come from homes where excessive drinking or alcoholism exists. The Alcoholism and Drug Addiction Research Foundation of Ontario, Canada, estimates that there are 100,000 alcoholics in Ontario at the present time.

People ask over and over again, Why does a person drink excessively when he is aware of the problems produced by his drinking? The answer is: The alcoholic is so filled with inner psychological pain that he must find immediate relief at any cost. Alcoholic anesthesia provides him with temporary relief from his inner suffering. The difficulty is that this relief demands a constantly increasing dosage of alcohol because of the tolerance which the body builds against it. Once a person's drinking has become excessive enough to disturb his family life, his vocational efficiency, and his financial stability, he is met with disapproval on every hand. This disapproval further lowers his self-respect and increases his inner psychological pain. His escape to alcohol then becomes even more necessary to him.

This, again, may indicate a need for outside help, and many well-known agencies are available to the public. There are also agencies to help the families of alcoholics in their understanding of the problem and their part in helping the alcoholic. If the alcoholic is willing to turn his life over to God's help and experiences a genuine conversion, the need for alcohol often disappears dramatically and immediately. The lives of many in the Christian church verify this fact. One of these people whom I have known intimately and have worked with closely is Lee Bryant, who tells her story in *Come Fill the Cup,* a book I recommend for alcoholics. The grace and forgiveness of God have so met the inner needs of such people that their psychological pain has been eased sufficiently to remove their need for the crutch of alcohol. Their craving for the bottle, which may have controlled them for many years, then disappears. There are other cases where a drinking problem has remained for a time after conversion. It is impossible to say that there has been insincerity in these cases, because only God knows the heart. This person should be encouraged to seek treatment for his emotional problems with the hope that, if there is a spiritual dimension present, it will provide the necessary motivation to use this help.

One necessary factor in the treatment of an alcoholic is that he have a genuine desire to rid himself of his drinking problem. Sometimes the family of such a person can help to produce this desire by firmly asserting that they will not allow him to disrupt their lives indefinitely. This is much more effective than the usual techniques of shaming, rejecting or belittling him, or the attempts to bribe, lecture or threaten him (without action). Alcoholics and their families are quite familiar with the emotional scenes which take place when the alcoholic is "at it again."

These scenes add guilt and rejection to the alcoholic's already long list of psychological hurts. Rather than asking, "Why are you doing this to us?" it is better to face him with his responsibility to seek help for his problem. If he refuses, his family may be forced to take action to protect their own lives. This can involve calling the police if he is violent, or going to family court if he is failing to support them. Such pressures motivate the alcoholic to seek help more than shaming or blaming does. If this kind of action is initated, it must not be withdrawn when the alcoholic pleads and promises to reform. Such ambivalence only makes matters worse.

A family in which there is an alcoholic would be wise to attend Alanon, the AA branch for families of alcoholics, where they will learn more about their part in the problem.

These are some of the patterns and problems of marriages needing professional help.

17

Does Marriage Improve with Age?

IN MY KITCHEN hangs a favorite print which a friend gave me years ago. It is a portrait of Noah and his wife after the flood, with the two faces superimposed upon a distant Mount Ararat. The deserted ark on the top of the mountain is circled by a rainbow. The Jewish faces pictured side by side are engraved with a network of wrinkles marking the toils and triumphs, the happiness and heartaches of a lifetime. As they turn their backs upon the distant ark, a strange calmness and light are in their eyes. To me, this picture represents a long and intimate marriage relationship. Having weathered many storms together, the couple now faces the future with a serenity unknown to youth. This serenity comes from a marriage relationship grown to full maturity in the soil of love—the love of a man and a woman for each other and for their God.

Some years ago I sensed the approach of this kind of marital relationship and wrote the following lines:

LOVE

I met Love in the Springtime,
  A flush upon her cheek,
Her song was bright and lilting,
  Her charm my heart did seek.

I skipped with Love through Summer,
  Our hearts did close entwine
While laughing on together
  Down the wooded paths of time.

I wove with Love in Autumn
  A lovely nest for two,
Content were we together
  'Though life's chill breezes blew.

> I dwelt with Love through Winter,
> Storms drove us closer still,
> Until one day with slower step
> We walked up Sunset Hill.

THE MIDDLE-AGE CRISIS

After the initial adjustments of marriage, the very busy years of child-bearing and child-rearing follow. The husband is establishing himself in his job or profession; the wife is preoccupied with the many demands of mothering. Suddenly, someday, the man will discover that he has reached most of his vocational and financial goals, and the woman will sense that her children no longer want her mothering. At first these discoveries will cause panic and the desire to run back to the challenging years before forty.

But soon the mature person will be able to change gears, although a temporary time of difficulty may be encountered during the forties while readjustment is taking place. Women are particularly affected since they are often experiencing the physical difficulties of the menopause. Men may also encounter emotional stress and depression as a result of a similar phase called the climacteric. Added to this pressure there may be difficulties encountered by the couple because of the adjustment problems or waywardness of their children, now in their late teens or early twenties.

All of these stresses of middle age unite the couple more than ever if they already have a well-adjusted marriage. If not, these difficulties may become sources of marital discord.

In his book, *The Revolt of the Middle Aged Man,* Edmund Bergler, a medical doctor, describes in detail the conflicts of some men during middle age. He notes that "man's middle-age revolt—the sudden discontent with everything (including marriage, professional duties, conventional pleasures) befalling men in the middle age—is a sad story of *an emotional second adolescence.*"[1] Then he describes how a man in this conflict longs to live life over again, feeling that he could avoid all of his past mistakes.

The wife of such a man is his most valuable asset if she remains by his side, a loyal, patient and understanding person. But this is usually difficult for her because she is also going through a time of personal adjustment and physical change resulting from the menopause and the growth of her children to independence.

Both men and women during this time are more than normally susceptible to fear, depression and pessimism. Each needs the other's loving concern more than ever. Often a medical doctor can help a couple over this crisis with medication which helps to rectify their hormonal imbalance.

Marriage After Forty-Five

After the passing of this time of emotional stress, marriage partners begin what is described by Dr. Marion Hilliard in her book, *A Woman Doctor Looks at Life and Love,* as the best years of their lives.[2]

The couple now have raised their children and are reaping the rewards of seeing them succeeding in a life of their own. These mates with no children to support now have a greater measure of financial security. Socially they are surrounded by a circle of friends who, like themselves, are free to enjoy the pleasures of community activities and good fellowship. Their strains in succeeding are fewer because they are established by their previous efforts and are experienced in their fields of endeavor. Some of their responsibilities can be relinquished to younger hands, which frees them to fulfill their personal needs in individual pursuits.

The marriage relationship at this stage of life can be an easy and comfortable union, free from competition or anxiety. Characterized by warm acceptance, kindly romanticism, and friendly banter, the mature marriage relationship becomes one of deeply rooted satisfaction. It is enhanced by the overtones of companionship with grown children and the spontaneous affection of grandchildren. If anyone has told you that the romance of early marriage is the best, don't believe them. There is no joy like the serene happiness of a mature marriage, mellowed by the stress of mutual suffering and the sharing of mutual joys. The two are one in a deep sense later in life, and yet they have never been so free to be themselves. Both are secure in a love which has stood the test of years.

This is marriage at its best—marriage come of age. The cream of the marital relationship rises to the top in the years after fifty. Both partners are enriched with happy memories and hopeful expectations. I have even seen marriages which could not be called close in the earlier years, grow into a mutually satisfying union when the partners were left alone to enjoy each other in an exclusive home relationship.

I doubt if Margaret Mead, the famous American anthropologist, can convince the older generation that marriage is on its way out. With all of its faults and weaknesses, marriage can still be the most satisfying of human relationships. The Communists tried free love but within a few years were happy to revert back to marriage.

Part IV

YOU AND YOUR CHILDREN

18

We Have a New Baby!

WHAT A HIGHLIGHT a baby is in life's experiences! During nine months of pregnancy the young couple have shared their anticipation. Daily they draw closer together through their mutual planning for the new baby. The day arrives and the mother experiences a new ecstasy as her newborn child is placed in her eager arms. To describe the wonder of that moment defies all words. It is like Paul's description of spiritual birth—unspeakable.

A baby cannot communicate verbally but he gets the "welcome" message emotionally. If there is resentment, rejection and disharmony between his parents, his arrival may cause apprehension instead of joy. He gets this message too, for he feels the tension and anxiety in his mother. Perhaps her husband has not given the warm support which she needs to prepare her for mothering their child.

THE IMPORTANCE OF EARLY MOTHERING

It is said that during the nine months previous to birth, a child receives his physical being, and during the nine months following birth, a child receives his emotional being. During the first two years of life, love is very much a one-way street. The mother gives love in the close contacts with her baby. He receives security from the comforting sound of her voice, the firm embrace of her arms, the loving smile in her eyes, and the warm milk from her breast. The cooing and play that go on between a mother and her infant child may seem like nonsense to an uninformed onlooker, but they are really an emotional communication which says to him, "Welcome, I love you. You don't need to be afraid." Many psychiatrists now believe that much anxiety and inability to form trustful relationships are rooted in failure to find emotional satisfaction during infancy.

It is evident that when a mother feels insecure and unloved in her marital relationship, she will find it hard to be the relaxed, emotionally spontaneous person needed to feed the emotional hungers of her newborn child. Husbands sometimes feel that they have no part in nurturing infants, failing to see that indirectly they contribute greatly to the success or failure of their child's first mothering experiences.

Dr. John Bowlby in his book *Child Care and the Growth of Love* gives convincing evidence of the importance of early mothering. This book, prepared from a United Nations study of maternal deprivation, depicts the failure of deprived children to form meaningful relationships later in life. He describes the victims of *total* maternal deprivation as feelingless individuals totally incapable of loving relationships with others.[1]

Although few people experience *total* maternal deprivation, there are many whose early mothering is much less than ideal. Bowlby's study should cause us to set aside any plans which would involve an infant in lengthy or frequent periods of separation from its mother. If careful attention is given to the mothering role until a child is two years old, a good foundation is laid and separation anxiety in the child is not as great as before that age.

The Two Antagonistic Drives of Infancy

At birth a child has two needs—the need to be loved, and the need to strike out against unpleasant situations in his environment—to be aggressive. When unmet, the need to be loved even causes poor physical development. It has been found that when babies have been given good institutional care with no mothering, they do not develop well physically or emotionally.

Because of this, many hospitals where babies are required to stay in care for prolonged periods have instituted a simulated mothering program. Babies are held and cuddled to ensure their healthy development. Some maternity wards have now adopted the rooming-in system where babies are kept in the rooms with their mothers and are always available to them to receive comfort and cuddling when they cry.

A baby's need to be aggressive is expressed in crying, sucking, restlessness and fretting when he is physically or psychologically uncomfortable. Early in life these two drives—the need to be loved and the need to assert oneself—are antagonistic. Later in life, an individual is able to reconcile the two drives to support a common goal.

A young child of two fears that if he expresses or even feels aggression he will lose his parent's love. This conflict is the source of much infantile anxiety. Later in life when he matures he will learn how to reconcile the two drives until they become mutually reinforcing. Let me illustrate:

Freddie is two years old and is playing in the same room with his sister, age three. He decides that he wants his sister's doll so he asserts himself and takes it forcibly from her. In so doing, he makes her angry and she hits him. Now he has found life filled with frustration and conflict. He wants to be loved by his sister and treated kindly, but he also wants her doll and has a need to assert himself to get it. But in so doing he fears that he has lost her love. The fear is even greater if the offended person is the mother, because she is the one who feeds him.

RECONCILING ANTAGONISTIC DRIVES

Eighteen years later, Fred is a youth of twenty. Having matured, he has learned to reconcile his need to be loved and his need to be aggressive. Now he sees that his sister has a car and he wants one too. Instead of stealing her car, he works overtime and saves all the money he can. Finally he buys himself a car. He has learned how to satisfy his desires by being aggressive in a socially acceptable way. Now he is able to get what he wants without disturbing the goodwill of his sister. His aggression is channeled into increased effort at his job.

The training of a child should satisfy his need to be loved and also his need to be aggressive. To do this there must be a careful balance between gratification and frustration. It is sad to see young children whose parents make unrealistic demands upon them, causing excessive frustration. If a child encounters too much anxiety when he expresses his drive to be loved or when he expresses his drive to be aggressive, he will deny these needs and thereby distort his personality.

The Training Period—Ages Two and Three

The last stage of infancy, while the child is two and three, is one of the most difficult for a child because there is so much training involved in developing behavior which is acceptable in our culture. Toilet training is more demanding here than in many other countries. In China, for example, a child merely squats and relieves himself wherever he is, for his split pants are designed for his convenience and no one finds this act offensive. Traffic hazards and the fast pace of city life add further pressures upon North American infants. Therefore, unnecessary frustrations must be removed to make the training period more bearable. In the homes of infants it is wise to clear the decks of unnecessary trinkets so our demands upon them will not be greater than their ability to comply. Long periods of waiting for food, exercise and other gratifications should be avoided.

If environmental pressures are too great at this stage, a child may develop such symptoms as thumb-sucking, bed-wetting, biting, nightmares, temper tantrums, refusal to eat, or purposeful soiling. His frustration will be expressed by a generous use of the word *no*. Take a look at Hazel and Hubert if you want to see two results of extreme parental control:

Hazel and Hubert—Opposite Children of Overfrustration

Hazel is a quiet young woman who becomes confused and embarrassed whenever she is asked an opinion. Because of her faithfulness and efficiency in the office where she works, she received a promotion to a supervisory position. But Hazel fell apart because she found it impossible to direct others. Having been punished so severely for any aggressive act during childhood, she now experiences great guilt and anxiety whenever she asserts herself. Hazel's domineering and overly strict mother gave her many restrictions and few gratifications during childhood. She rebelled against these frustrations and when her mother punished her severely, she feared the loss of her mother's love and felt guilty about self-assertion. Gradually she learned to submit to every demand, and only then did she feel accepted and loved by her demanding mother. Now she is a faint shadow of the person she might have been.

Hubert, her brother, reacted in the opposite way and became a detached individual who cares little about relationships. A successful businessman who drives a hard bargain with everyone he meets, he is so aggressive and harsh in his treatment of others that his personal relationships are unsuccessful. Hubert has repressed his need to be loved, preferring to satisfy his aggressive drives instead.

How sad that Hazel and Hubert were not given a good balance of gratification and frustration so that neither of these unhealthy solutions would be necessary.

THELMA—CHILD OF OVERPERMISSIVENESS

The opposite extreme to overfrustration is overpermissiveness. This approach to child-raising gives children too much gratification and not enough control to teach them the art of healthy socialization. We have all observed the fretful, objectionable little monster whose every desire has been gratified by indulgent parents.

Thelma was just such a child. Her parents treated her like a queen, waiting on her as she shouted commands. They believed in full self-expression with no controls, and Thelma became an expert at expressing herself in no uncertain tones. At school she continued to demand full attention and when the teachers tried to discipline her, her mother interfered. After changing schools and courses several times, she dropped out. At seventeen she became pregnant and married prematurely, but her husband found it unbearable to accept her demands and soon the marriage ended in divorce. Now Thelma is back home with her mother, who is still her humble slave, and the grandchild is being spoiled by her grandmother's permissiveness.

These are some of the principles behind the successful nurturing of infants and some of the results of the excesses of permissiveness or frustration. No wonder the Scriptures instruct parents, "Do not irritate and provoke your children to anger—do not exasperate them to resentment—but rear them [tenderly] in the training and discipline and the counsel and admonition of the Lord.[2]

Given balanced doses of gratification and frustration and the emotional support of loving parents, a child will pass the difficult training period and enter the quieter stage of early childhood.

19

Our Baby Is Growing Up!

CHILDHOOD is the happy period between foot-stamping infancy and uncertain adolescence. During these years from four to eleven, success is dependent on diminishing parental control and growing self-control. It is a period of learning to socialize, first in the family group and then in the peer group.

EARLY CHILDHOOD—AGES FOUR AND FIVE

The lovable four- and five-year-olds are a bright relief from the hot-tempered two- and three-year-olds. By four, a child has normally discovered that there are other people in his world who have needs and desires of their own, and that mother has other interests besides him. Father for the first time takes on real signfiicance. Marital disharmony affects children of these ages more than at any time. A child's sex identification, which normally takes place at this time, is dependent upon his knowledge that his parents love each other. If the little girl knows that her father loves her mother, she will want to be like mother so he will love her too. It is during these years, therefore, that little girls adore their fathers and mimic their mothers. Playing house is all part of becoming a woman, and the unconscious motive behind this sex identification is to gain her father's love.

A little boy plays the same game in reverse. Driving a pretend car and chasing intruders are his attempts to be like dad so that mother will love him as she loves dad. If mother does not seem to love dad, there is no reason to be like him. With both boys and girls, therefore, marital conflict can be one cause of poor sex identification. Because of their need to find their place in the family, four- and five-year-olds are perhaps the most lovable of all children.

Preoccupation with sexual differences is common at this age. Sometimes sexual curiosity will cause a little boy to expose himself to a girl and to ask the same favor of her. He will be preoccupied with investigating and handling his own sexual organs. If parents become alarmed and react harshly or anxiously, the child will develop excessive anxiety over sexual matters. If dealt with unemotionally, these incidents will pass without harm.

"Where do babies come from?" is a common question at this age. The arrival of a little brother or sister encourages such inquiry. Simple, unconcerned answers are sufficient, for making a big production out of sex education is both unnatural and unnecessary.

At five, junior goes off to school, a transition which goes smoothly after a few days if junior's mother is emotionally ready to let him go into his own world.

MIDDLE CHILDHOOD—AGES SIX, SEVEN AND EIGHT

The child now turns from his preoccupation with his family and his sex to the outer world. No longer the tenderhearted, loving individual he was at four or five, he now shows signs of entering the rough-and-ready stage of middle childhood. He still needs a secure parental relationship because "making it" in the child's world is a struggle with many conflicts and frustrations. Giving up his personal aims for the aims of the play group will be difficult. He wants to pitch for his ball team even if he loses the game for them. Gradually group pressures will teach him to accept personal restrictions for the common good.

Play is of great value in teaching a child to socialize and cooperate. He learns to control his impulses to gain group favor and acceptance. His ego is often battered and sore from the ridicule and criticism which he receives in the give and take of play. If he is clumsy or fat or smaller than his playmates, his frustration will be greater. Parental interference will humiliate him further and make him feel more inadequate.

The six-to-eight-year-old needs warm acceptance at home, with plenty of ego-building encouragement to offset frustrations at play and at school. In my opinion, too much adult supervision in the child's world defeats the purpose of play. Children need to be left alone to learn from the play group the lessons of cooperation and sharing.

The chief difficulties at home will be in the matters of grooming and punctuality. Extreme preoccupation with play will make these children unaware of time and appearance.

Competitive games and rough play will change the devoted five-year-old boy into the rough-and-tumble eight-year-old. Since this change is difficult for his mother to accept, a good father relationship is important at this age.

Girls also have their conflicts and become involved in bitter quarrels with their playmates. They struggle over choosing a president for their club or getting the first turn at a new game. As time passes, girls too will learn to cooperate with the group. They will have more interest in grooming than boys but still not enough to please their fathers.

Recognition is the great need of this period, so crticism should be limited and praise generous. These children need time to dawdle, to dream and to think. Demands of the classroom and the playground leave them tense, and home should be a place to relax. If demanding parents goad them into constant activity, they will react with anger and frustration. Their only escape will be found in such pastimes as dawdling in the bathroom or daydreaming on the garage roof. Here they can relax in privacy away from parental control.

Poor adjustment during this period will result in withdrawal from play groups, truancy from school, petty thieving, irritability, destructiveness, excessive daydreaming and fantasy. All of this is rebellion against too much regimentation. Children vary in nature and therefore in their ability to tolerate frustration.

Dr. Irene M. Josselyn in her book *The Psychosocial Development of Children* notes that "punishment is at times necessary in order to sharpen the necessity for conformity in regard to important issues. . . . Punishment is most meaningful to the child when it is in proportion to the misdemeanor rather than in proportion to the parent's irritation. Most children will accept reasonable restrictions if they have the repeated reassuring experience of having their own desires considered when major decisions are not at stake."[1] If they are given responsibility for decisions beyond their capacity, they will become confused, insecure and unhappy.

Later Childhood—Ages Nine, Ten, and Eleven

The later childhood period has been called "the adulthood of childhood." If the early years of childhood are passed successfully, the nine-to-eleven-year-old will be a well-adjusted, happy, and fairly cooperative individual. Under these conditions he will present fewer problems to his parents than at any other age. But if his previous adjustment has been poor, symptoms of delinquency, withdrawal or hostility will be evident at this age.

These years of childhood give parents their greatest opportunity to instruct their children mentally, spiritually and socially. Perhaps this is why it is called the age of decision. Adolescence seems to nullify all the efforts of parents during childhood; but if a good foundation has been built, results will be seen later.

20

What Does It Mean to "Train Up a Child" Physically, Mentally and Spiritually?

A VERSE FROM PROVERBS is often quoted glibly: "Train up a child in the way he should go: and when he is old, he will not depart from it."[1] Some interpret this as "Take your child to church, and when he is old he will not turn out wrong." Others think the verse means that training a child is very much like training a dog. To them the verse means, "Whenever your child does something you don't want him to do, punish him, and when he is old he will act just as you have trained him to act." The Amplified Bible adds new meaning to the verse: "Train up a child in the way he should go and in keeping with his individual gift or bent."[2] A verse of Scripture used to describe Jesus at the age of twelve throws further light on the meaning of training a child.

THE BOY JESUS ILLUSTRATES THE PROCESS OF CHILD-TRAINING

When God's Son, Jesus Christ, took a human form, He was born into a family. Mary was chosen to give Him mothering, and Joseph, though not His biological father, gave Him human fathering.

In the Bible we read this simple description of the result of their care of the boy Jesus: "And Jesus increased in wisdom and stature, and in favour with God and man."[3] This, in one comprehensive sentence, is the task of Christian parenthood. Broken down into our terms, it means the child matured physically in stature, mentally in wisdom, socially in favor with man, and spiritually in favor with God. These should be our goals in training children.

To enter into an explanation of how the Son of God could mature is not our purpose, except to say that, while He was the Son of God, He became the son of man at His birth. As the son of man He required and responded to parental nurturing.

PHYSICAL MATURITY

Because our culture overemphasizes the care of the body, there is little need to comment further. However, much of a mother's time is spent on the physical care of her family. During each child's "growing up" years, she will do about 1,500 washings, prepare about 6,000 meals, spend numerous sleepless nights, take thousands of weary steps, and patch up a variety of calamities both great and small. She cannot hope to be really free from child-raising responsibilities until she is about forty years old. This requires that a mother be dedicated to her task. She needs the spirit of the mother who placed this sign over her kitchen sink: "Divine services here, three times daily."

Helping a child mature physically not only involves providing for his basic needs of food, clothing, shelter and rest. It involves helping him to learn control of his physical appetites. Many adults are hampered by their shoddy health habits and by their inability to control their physical hungers. Paul, although he had chronic health problems, endured severe physical hardship and accomplished much for God because he had learned to keep his body under subjection.[4] We need to teach our children to make servants of their bodies rather than masters.

Father as well as mother should have a part in this training but, his chief role will be that of providing materially. It is estimated that each child will cost him three years' salary.

MENTAL MATURITY

Mary's child matured not only physically, but also mentally.

At the age of twelve He astounded the Ph.D.'s at the temple with His understanding and answers.[5]

Mental maturity is not produced by constantly nagging a child about his homework. Learning was once looked upon as a passive acceptance of knowledge, but now it is understood as an aggressive act. There is no real learning without first an eagerness to learn. The preservation and stimulation of this faculty, which is natural to all mentally capable children, constitute one of the goals of mental maturity. The desire to learn can be thwarted by an overly controlling parent. If the learning adventures of a toddler are constantly thwarted by oversupervision, a child will develop guilt over the aggressive act of learning. A social worker put it well: "Behind every underachieving young man is a mother who talks too much."

Repeated angry reactions to the questions of a five-year-old will eventually discourage his quest for knowledge. His third-degree methods are irritating, especially when his parents are busy. No parent can be expected to always respond patiently. I remember hearing about a child who was "helping" his father repair a doorknob. He kept up a constant barrage of questions until his father remarked with exasperation, "You are just one big question mark!"

The boy was silent for a long time and the father thought he had stopped his questions. Then came the next one: "Daddy, if I'm a question mark, how can I sit on my dot?"

Children have a right to be heard and answered patiently as much as possbile. When they grow beyond our ability to answer, we need to look for books or informed people who can supply information for them.

A parent who wants to encourage learning will surround his child with a mentally enriched environment—a home where stimulating books are read and where ideas can be expressed and discussed without fear of ridicule or rejection. One speaker observed that an unstored mind cannot be inspired.

It is also important to help children develop some objectivity so that they will think with their minds and not only with their hearts. Too often facts are distorted by emotions and prejudices. One man who was exploited by his landlord now suspects that all landlords are crooks. Then there are the people who have met one insincere Christian and now consider all Christians to be phony. Do the young people from our Christian homes learn to think objectively or with prejudices? None of us can be completely objective because subjective feelings enter into everyone's view of reality. However, parents should endeavor to be objective and unprejudiced, thus giving an example to their children.

One of the greatest hindrances to influencing a child's thinking is a parent who feels he must know all the answers and be right all the time. A child needs to be given the concept that human understanding is limited, and that God alone is all-knowing. This principle, acknowledged early in life, will protect growing minds from that sophistication which has gripped the academic community of our day.

This situation is no surprise to God. Paul taught that in later times men would be "heady, highminded," or as another translation puts it, "inflated with self-conceit."[6] In an earlier day the founders of Yale, Harvard and most other universities had the mental humility to acknowledge God and His revelation of truth in the Bible as superior to human investigation and thought. This is illustrated by Edwin Rian in his book *Christianity and American Education*,[7] where he quotes from the charters of early universities. When Christian parents establish their children in this mental attitude early in life, it makes them more selective in what they accept as truth. Many Christian educators today are convinced that Christian parents should provide separate schools based on the Christian ethic because they are convinced that when we allow our children to be educated in an atmosphere of secularism and atheism we are not training them in the way they should go. This viewpoint is food for thought.

SPIRITUAL MATURITY

Spiritual maturity is sometimes slow in developing, especially when a young person has matured mentally, physically and socially. An immature, inadequate young person who has little self-confidence will sometimes follow mechanically after the beliefs of his Christian parents, while a youth who has been taught to think for himself will flounder in unbelief for a time. It is significant that some of the greatest leaders of today's church have, like Paul, been rebels during their youth.

What can a parent do to help a child mature spiritually? John tells us that those who receive Christ are born not of blood (heredity) nor of the will of the flesh (human effort) or of the will of man (human persuasion) but of God.[8] We cannot manipulate our children into spiritual decisions; we can only teach them what God is like and how they can know Him. Then we can pray that this teaching will take root and grow into living faith under the influence of the Holy Spirit.

The parent who uses the pressures of grief, shame or hurt pride to produce guilt in an unbelieving young person, only forces a surface conformity to church standards. That parent is jeopardizing the spiritual maturity of his child and fostering either hypocrisy or open rebellion.

Sometimes religion clouds the person of God with a host of taboos, traditions and inconsistencies. Then we wonder why our young people give up trying to discover the basic issues of Christianity and write the church off as having no meaning in everyday living. Instead of clouding the issues about God, let us clarify them.

TEACH CHILDREN ABOUT GOD

THAT GOD IS ABSOLUTE LOVE

When no one understands us, God does. He cares for us more than parents or friends. If we teach this truth, our children will remember it on days when they feel empty, lonely and misunderstood. Then they will want God.

THAT GOD IS ABSOLUTE TRUTH

God does not need to learn or discover, for He knows all

things, even the hidden thoughts of the heart. God's knowledge never needs revision because it is not limited by time or space. He sees the essence of things past, present and future. The guidance of this all-knowing God is available to all who will be humble enough to want it. Given this concept, our children will turn to God in the midst of perplexity.

THAT GOD IS ABSOLUTE RIGHTEOUSNESS

Men's standards, which are socially based, change from generation to generation, but God has a perfect and immutable standard. We have only a tarnished and partial approximation of right and wrong, while His righteousness is full, penetrating even to the motives of the heart. Therefore He is qualified to judge sin. He is just in all His judgments, and with His righteousness He offers mercy through His Son who did not come "to condemn the world; but that the world through him might be saved."[9] This knowledge will make it easier for young people to confess their sin and humbly trust in God.

THAT GOD IS ABSOLUTE POWER

God upholds "all things by the word of his power."[10] The one who made man in His image is the only one who can give him the power to live the spontaneous life—the Bible calls it "abundant life." When life becomes too much, your child's mind will return to this teaching and long for deliverance from the bondage of his own depraved nature.

THAT GOD IS ALL-PRESENT

There is no speech or language where God's voice is not heard.[11] He has always been "there" to meet the rebels. In the success of the palace or the depravity of the pigpen, in the skepticism of the Damascus road, or under the weeping willows of the land of exile, God met these rebels when they were ready to return. After they gave themselves up to His love, His presence became a comfort instead of a terror. He is the God who comes alongside to help. Sometimes only a trip to the "far country" will bring our children to this discovery.

TEACH CHILDREN THE WAY TO GOD

Then teach children the way to God—through His Son. A young Union soldier is reported to have requested leave from active duty during the darkest hours of the Civil War because his wife was dying at home. His request was refused. Going to the White House, he tried to reach President Lincoln personally but was refused entrance by a sentry at the gate. Sitting on the White House wall, he considered his plight. A small boy accosted him and, for want of sympathy, he told the boy his story. The lad cupped his hands to his mouth and yelled, "Daddy." The tall figure of Lincoln came out the front door and, following the voice to the wall, heard the soldier's plea and granted the leave. Lincoln's son found access for the needy soldier. No need to enlarge the lesson! Teach children that Jesus Christ is the way to God.

21

What Does It Mean to "Train Up a Child" Socially?

MANY PEOPLE, in and out of the church, are hindered by their social immaturity. They enter adulthood dragging their teens behind them. How can we as parents help our children become mature adults? There are certain concepts which, when taken together, describe a mature person. These we need to teach by precept and example.

THE CONCEPT OF SELF AND OTHERS

At birth every human being is the center of his whole world —the pivot upon which everything turns. Before we become socially mature, we must learn to view ourselves not as a pivot but as a cog. We need to learn cooperation with others. In this age of individualism, when so many view everything in the light of their own satisfactions, it is refreshing to meet people whose focus is on others rather than on self. The Bible urges Christians to grow in this concept: "Love one another . . . giving precedence and showing honor to one another."[1] "Let each of you . . . be concerned for not [merely] his own interests, but also each for the interests of others."[2]

We do a child an injustice when we fail to teach him consideration for others by restraining his selfish acts. Although our expectations must be suited to the age and disposition of the child, "other-centeredness" can be taught. When a child learns to be thoughtful of others, he has opened a door to lifelong satisfaction in happy social relationships.

THE CONCEPT OF MINE AND YOURS

Other-centeredness will create respect for the possessions of others. There will be a clear line between "mine" and "yours" when children are trained in this concept from the cradle.

One afternoon while riding a bus, I observed a chattering four-year-old bobbing about on the seat beside her mother. Suddenly her bright eyes sighted a sparkling trinket dangling from the hinge of the seat. It looked like a broken earring. "Mommy, look what I found!" she shrieked. Her mother smiled and said, "That's nice, dear, but that belongs to someone else. I think you should take it to the driver."

The girl made her way reluctantly to the front of the bus and gave it to the driver. He examined it carefully and put it back in her hand. "I don't think anyone will want that. It seems to be broken," he said. "You can have it."

The child returned, gleeful over her treasure. I suppose some passengers thought, *How Silly! That woman made a big fuss about nothing.*

Perhaps without knowing it she was teaching her child to respect the property of others. One look at the enormity of our national theft makes it clear that these ethics are not being widely taught. The concept of "What's yours is mine, and what's mine is my own" seems to be increasingly popular. The Bible discourages a self-centered disrespect for the property of others: "Let the thief steal no more, but rather let him be industrious, making an honest living with his own hands, so that he may be able to give to those in need."[3] Mature unselfishness places the emphasis on giving, not taking.

But there are other ways of taking which are much more damaging than stealing another man's possessions. We can steal his right to be an individual and to develop in his own way. How many parents or marriage partners have done this. It is ironical that often children who have been victims of this kind of emotional rape present a pattern of stealing—sometimes taking the possessions of the very parent who has exploited their individuality. Every human being has a right to be a person who is different and separate from all other individuals. Not even parenthood or marriage gives us the right to exploit another person. How often we have heard parents say in anger, "Why can't you be like your brother?" Or perhaps more often, "Why can't you be like your sister?" Or conversely they say, "You're just like your Aunt Lucy!" and the child knows that Aunt Lucy is the skeleton in the family closet. To force a child into any mold—whether the mold be good or bad—is wrong. Domination is never justified, even by a good end. Incidentally, the end that may seem good is nothing but surface conformity, a shell of a person playing the part that a well-meaning parent has demanded of him.

If the Son of God would not invade the privacy of a human personality without an invitation to enter, why should we? He is pictured as knocking at a closed door, waiting for the owner to open it. Again we see Him wanting to gather the people of Jerusalem under His wings as a hen gathers her chickens, but restraining himself because of the barrier of their human wills. "And ye would not," He lamented.[4] He *could* have forced His way, but He *would* not. He was hindered, not by their unwillingness, but by His own character.

Then there is the whole area of privacy—a human right which should be carefully guarded. Sometimes parents violate a child's privacy, prying into his secrets, eavesdropping on his conversations, and refusing him a place of his very own where he can retreat and be alone with his own thoughts. The same parents will "tell all" to neighbors and friends, even in a child's hearing. Later they are astonished when their children escape into lying and fantasy and refuse to confide in any adult. Such parents do not see their children as separate selves with rights, possessions and privacies of their own. Because of this attitude, too many Christians fail to see the difference between influencing their children and dominating them.

THE CONCEPT OF DEPENDENCE AND INDEPENDENCE

At birth a child is totally dependent on its mother, emotionally and physically. As he grows, that dependence diminishes until adulthood when the "apron strings" should be completely cut. He will then experience interdependence with other individuals, and enjoy a reciprocal relationship in which each person keeps his individuality and yet contributes to the needs of the other. This is quite different from a dependent relationship in which one person continually feeds upon another to meet his emotional needs. When this happens it becomes unnecessary and even impossible for the dependent person to develop his own inner resources.

How can a parent help a child move from complete dependence to independence? One way is to refrain from doing for your child anything that he is capable of doing for himself. The other side involves not expecting him to do for himself what he is incapable of doing, thus destroying his self-confidence. To establish his capabilities at various ages, you may need to talk to other parents and children. Books are also helpful, especially a paperback called *The Gesell Institute's Child Behavior* by Frances L. Ilg, a medical doctor, and Louise Bates Ames, Ph.D.[5]

Behind emotional dependence in older children there is usually one parent's need to foster it. This parent, who usually has never achieved emotional independence himself, finds that an independent child is too great a threat to his own emotional security. This kind of parent is at one time critical and belittling, robbing the child of confidence; and at another time, pampering and protective, tying the child to him. This inconsistency is damaging to a growing personality.

If this seems to be happening between yourself and your child, try to avoid being critical; and if he is disciplined by your mate or by a teacher, do not allow yourself to fly to his defense. A hostility-dependency relationship between yourself and your child will damage both of you. If your mate is more consistent and mature, let him handle crisis situations. Family counselling could be helpful.

Normally a parent who is emotionally secure will be able to gradually withdraw his control from a child as he grows older. It is unfortunate that some young people have to stage a major revolt before their parents discover that they have been holding the reins too tightly. No wonder the prophet Jeremiah said, "It is good for a man that he bear the yoke in his youth."[6]

THE CONCEPT OF COMPLETE IDENTIFICATION VERSUS AUTONOMY

Close to the concept of dependence and independence is the identity crisis when a child moves from complete identity with the parents to personal autonomy. Some never quite make this leap and are always a rubber stamp of their parents, with no selfhood or autonomy of their own. Their opinions, attitudes and convictions are all secondhand. Spiritually they are what Bob Pierce calls "God's grandchildren." Our evangelical pews are full of them: the elder brothers who never left home but are devoid of deep feelings for either the Father or the prodigal.

At birth we have no concept of selfhood. It is a great discovery when the new baby first notices his kicking feet and sees that he has a physical self which he can control. Later he discovers a psychological self which is different and separate from his parents. This identity crisis can come at different ages and under varying circumstances.

I remember seeing an interview with the great psychoanalyst Carl Gustov Jung televised by the British Broadcasting Corporation just prior to his death. He recounted the occasion when, as an eleven-year-old schoolboy he suddenly and clearly became aware of his own identity. As he walked to school one day he realized that he was a person who was different and separate from his parents, and therefore responsible for his own actions. He recounted how the insight both frightened and thrilled him with its importance. Perhaps everyone's experience is not always as clear as in Jung's case, but self-discovery must happen for all. A growing self-awareness will accompany the maturing process throughout life. Only by the insight of selfhood can one become socially autonomous. Then one's relationships are not like the grasp of a drowning man reaching for his rescuer, or the frenzy of a cornered man resisting his attacker, or the flight of a hunted man seeking a place to hide. These images describe the extremes of relationship patterns—those who move desperately *toward people* to bolster their failing ego, those who move defensively *against people* to protect themselves against suspected attackers, and those who move anxiously *away from people,* fearing discovery of a self-image which they themselves abhor.[7]

Your child needs to be a person in his own right, and only you can build into him in childhood the confidence and self-esteem that he needs. He will then find inner emotional resources which will enable him to enjoy happy creative relationships with others.

The Concept of Now and Later

A young child has no ability to project his plans or desires into the future. If you offer him the choice of a small sucker now or a big one tomorrow, he will take the small one now. He has not yet learned to endure the tensions of waiting. A baby does not lie in his crib and say to himself, "I am very hungry for my two A.M. bottle, but my poor mother is very tired and needs her sleep. I must therefore endure these hunger pains as long as I can so she can get her rest." An infant has no such concept. To mature, a child must learn how to restrain his desires for later fulfillment. It is a hard lesson.

I recall how hard this was at the age of ten for my rather impetuous son. When he received his weekly allowance one summer Saturday, he told me that he was going to buy a pair of swimming goggles. I inquired as to the cost and found it to be his complete allowance. I told him that it would be up to him but pointed out that if he bought the goggles he would have no money to go swimming at the pool. I recommended that he wait and save part of his money for the goggles, while using the rest for his swimming. After two or three weeks he would then have both.

"No, I'm going to buy them today," he said, and he did just that.

I don't think there has been a hotter July week in my experience. It was difficult to watch David sitting in the backyard wearing his swimming goggles while his friends went off to the pool with their towels over their shoulders. After many similar experiences over a number of years, David, now a father himself, learned not to sacrifice the future on the altar of the present.

Inability to wait for things has caused untold damage to lives. Unmarried young people can't wait until marriage to have sexual relations, and a seventeen-year-old becomes pregnant. A young man can't wait to have a car, so he quits school in the middle of grade ten and goes to work, jeopardizing his economic future. An immature married couple can't wait for all the luxuries which their older neighbors enjoy, so they go deeply into debt.

These people have not learned to accept the tensions of waiting for the fulfillment of their desires. The reason? Their parents never denied them anything. How can Johnny be expected to wait for things if he has always had everything his little heart desired?

This is a biblical principle, for the Bible talks about the value of sowing a good harvest now and reaping later.[8] It tells us to cast our bread upon the waters now and find it after many days,[9] and to lay up treasures now and enjoy riches later.[10]

THE CONCEPT OF EFFORT AND REWARD

Close to the concept of now and later is the idea of effort and reward. Some children are never given the thrill of putting forth effort and receiving the rewards of that effort—not only material reward but the deep satisfactions of accomplishment.

I suspect that by the way some parents complain about work, they have never personally enjoyed the thrill of accomplishment, or the rewards of a job well done. No wonder we see so much inefficiency in our culture when so many "turn off" on Monday and come alive on the weekend. Young people need to learn good work habits during childhood so that they will not expect rewards without effort.

The Bible says we should serve in our daily work, "not with eyeservice, as men-pleasers; but as the servants of Christ, doing the will of God from the heart."[11] In other words, "Work whether the boss is looking or not."

There's another side to the coin. Not only is there the positive view of effort and reward but there is the negative concept of actions and consequences. Children need to learn that certain kinds of actions bring bad consequences. Many times mothers who have come to my office from the court in which their sons have been convicted of a crime, have tearfully asked, "Why would he do this when we have given him everything?"

Such mothers are answering their own question. A son who has been given everything has had no opportunity to develop responsible attitudes. Conversely, a youth who has never been allowed to reap the consequences of his own actions has had no opportunity to learn from his own mistakes. At home mother protected him from father's discipline. At school she shielded him from his teachers and managed an "out" for him when he was about to reap the consequences of his insolence and laziness. Perhaps the "out" involved a change in courses or transfer to another school. Now that his impulsive behavior has finally brought him to the court, he is beyond his mother's protection and, for the first time in his life, must reap his own consequences. How much better for him to learn about such consequences in his own home and thus avoid a criminal record.

"Train up a child" in its social implications involves teaching these all-important concepts of healthy social adjustment. They will be taught best by our living example.

Romans 12:1-2 says that we should give ourselves fully to the transforming power of God. It takes nineteen more verses to explain how we should express our Christianity in everyday life. These social concepts are in those verses.

Part V

YOU AND YOUR YOUNG PEOPLE

22

Are Teenagers Really Impossible?

WHEN MY CHILDREN were juniors—lovable, earnest, exuberant juniors—I wrote a little verse. It was really not written out of experience, but from pure heresay. I had heard so many parents sigh and say: "Wait till your children are in their teens."

This comment was usually followed by a list of complaints that made living with "teens" sound like the great tribulation. So—little wonder I penned the following lines:

> Whether in city
> Or rural seclusion,
> With children in "teens"
> You will live in confusion.

I almost dreaded the day we would put thirteen candles on a birthday cake, but that day came and went twice in our family. Life became a little complex at times, but it also became intensely enjoyable after I learned a few lessons.

The first thing I learned was to admit that I could be wrong about some things and my children right. Somehow we parents get the feeling that when our children reach thirteen, we lose something. Parents look back longingly to those gilded days when junior thought his five-foot-six dad was able to "lick" any man on the street—and proclaimed the same with boldness. Susie, at the same age, believed her pop had an inexhaustible bankroll. Her stories of "what my mom is going to buy me" would make even the boldest parent droop with humility. At thirteen, all is changed. Your offspring no longer sees you through the rose-colored glasses of childhood but with the microscopic accuracy of adulthood. Still being part child, he proclaims his impressions aloud. You will be jarred by his none-too-complimentary remarks about your figure, your cooking, your hair style and your language. The confidence you felt during the first twelve years of parenthood will melt, and you will be under the most critical scrutiny of your lifetime. If your ego is weak you will suffer feelings of inadequacy, but an understanding of what has taken place in your child will soften the blow.

This critical spirit is the budding of maturity. Your child is becoming an adult and his near-worship of his parents is fading. Now he is beginning to feel equal to you and independent so that he can view you with the critical eye of a contemporary. His security no longer rests on the childhood illusion that you are invincible and faultless. He is finding a new self-sufficiency deep within him and no longer needs to believe you are flawless.

At this awakening it will pay you to admit your weak points and be amused with him over your peculiarities. If you attempt in self-defense to restore the worshipful attitude of childhood, your child will only try harder to bring you down to size. Be thankful that he is developing, even if the symptoms are distressing. After all, who wants to be a fairy godmother for life? Blind devotion is flattering but not mature.

Only the other day I watched a father and his adoring daughter, age five, sit down at a table in a restaurant.

"What do you want, dear?" the father asked.

"Whatever you want, I want too," she replied with worship in her big brown eyes.

I had a mental picture of the same daughter at fifteen. Instead her actions will seem to say, "Whatever you want I don't want." I'm sure any father would miss such adoration.

For years you thought you were molding the life of your child—and you were. Suddenly overnight all your training seems to be gone with the wind of adolescence.

Johnny, who has always been exposed to good music, now calls it long-haired and prefers the hit parade. Carol, who had beautiful manners a few months ago, becomes positively crude in her habits. Her "slanguage" is anything but cultured, and the clutter she leaves behind her would keep a maid busy, full time. You will observe all this and a sickening sense of failure will overwhelm you. But after observation and consultation with other teenagers' parents you will discover that it is a common symptom. What is really happening is that your child is changing gears—from childhood to adulthood. Inexperience grinds the gears, but an understanding parent can help young people make the transition less painfully. Unfortunately, too many of us neither understand the process nor sense the need for it until a great deal of gear-stripping has gone on and resentment has built up in both parent and child.

These resentments would not be so common if parents knew that adolescence is a testing time, a time when children try the standards and ideals of their parents and finally either discard or accept them. Though it may look for a while as if your children will toss overboard everything you have taught them, they won't. That is—unless you thwart their testing motives too completely, and produce a general rebellion against everything for which you stand. If your beliefs and your way of life are worthwhile, and if you don't keep too tight a rein but allow your adolescent a little *harmless* experimentation, you will be happier and he will emerge with ideals and beliefs much like yours.

If you refuse to let your young person try his wings in harmless ways, he will find ways which may be harmful. So, if there is a harmless dress fad at school, go along with it. Enjoy it. It has a very curative purpose. However, remember that your child still needs your guidance. When he insists on testing moral principles, he needs a quiet man-to-man discussion of the consequences and, if he still insists on his own way, he needs a firm *no.* The latter may bring a storm, but it will protect him till he is ready to establish sound convictions of his own.

After all, who wants young people with secondhand convictions? Show them why you have certain convictions, and teach them from the experience of others what works best in everyday living. Where possible, let them experiment too. Consequences that are not too damaging will teach more than your lectures.

To produce young people with strong principles, we parents must be willing to allow some mistakes and failures—there are no better tutors. I remember when my boy failed his first year at high school. With urging and coaching we might have pushed him through, but we didn't. He learned two very important lessons about life that year: that success costs effort, and that failure can be overcome. His lost year was one of those successful failures of life. He now has a master's degree from Berkeley and holds a Phi Beta Kappa key for his efforts.

Besides learning to let our adolescents experiment, we will do well to realize the effectiveness of a positive suggestion rather than a negative command—especially in dealing with his tender spots. You see, every teenager has areas where he is very sore to criticism. When you hit these areas you may encounter a burst of resentment and hostility. One of these trouble spots is touched by any suggestion that he is not grown up, though he may look like it physically. Down deep inside he knows he is immature, but he wants desperately to hide it and greatly resents being treated like a child. The more you recognize his grown-up-ness, the less trouble you will have. This is done by taking him into your confidence, giving him responsibility, and even asking him advice about subjects on which he is better informed than you.

Many teenagers have gone out to do foolhardy things, morally, physically and socially, to prove their manhood or womanhood. Don't make this necessary. I believe our parents were wiser in this. When a boy in the 1920s put on long pants, he became a man and was expected to act like one. There was no need for him to rebel against convention to prove his manhood.

Besides this attack on our adolescents' immaturity, we often hurt him by reminding him of certain telltale physical signs of it. Everytime we reprimand the adolescent for his clumsiness or tease him about his awkwardness, we remind him that he is half child and half adult and unable to operate efficiently as either. His big feet and pimply face yell to all the world that he is not completely grownup, even though he is taller than his parents.

He would love to be rid of these telltale signs, so don't remind him of them.

Emotionally too, he does not always react in a grownup way. When things get out of hand emotionally he feels like a failure at maturing. Too often we parents pile a burden of guilt on top of his burden of failure at such times. Your adolescent will defend himself desperately if you attack him during these outbursts, but all the time he is filled with fears that he may never gain control of his emotions. Encourage him when the storm passes and try to show him more acceptable ways of handling life situations. And above all, don't use yourself as an example of virtue.

Most important of all, let your teenagers know that you love them just as they are. If *you* don't give them recognition and acceptance, the gang at the corner lunch counter or poolroom will. Remember always that they are not finished products, so don't expect too much. You'll find your teens quite lovable if you remember this. If they see reality in you, they will follow your guidance. They will want to become what you are, not what you pretend to be.

So, given a firm faith in God, a warm love from their parents, and a cheerful atmosphere of acceptance, most teenagers will emerge from the "great tribulation" better for it—and so will their parents.

23

What Are the Goals of Growing Up?

THE PRINCIPLE that no project is apt to succeed unless it has well-defined goals applies to growing up as much as to any other accomplishment. Since both young people and their parents often lack direction because their purposes are not clear, here are some specific goals of adolescence toward which both should aim:

THE GOAL OF EMOTIONAL MATURITY

By age eleven, children seem to be able to control their emotions fairly well, no longer indulging in the extreme outbursts of anger, excitement, disappointment, and tearful sadness so typical of infancy and early childhood. Parents begin to relax and feel that they have almost completed their task and that their children are capable of making their way in the world.

At thirteen the same parents discover that they are starting all over again. Their emotionally stable eleven-year-old is now the victim of the most violent and sudden mood swings. The outbursts of uncontrolled anger, unjustified excitement, and unexplained depression begin all over again. In fact, all three moods may follow in quick succession. Many parents end up in doctors' offices, fearing that their teenagers are emotionally ill. The same extremes of mood at other ages might indicate trouble, but in the teen years they are fairly common.

This situation makes the establishment of emotional maturity one of the adolescent goals. Overreacting emotionally to environmental stimuli is sometimes a sign of immaturity. Although some variation in emotional reaction is to be expected because of differences in temperament, emotional extremes drain one's nervous energy and some attempt should be made to control them. Parents can help reach this goal by controlling their own emotions. Some families seem to be on an emotional binge periodically when everyone in the house vents his feelings, expressing all sorts of strong emotions. Shouting, tears, harsh words, and irrational threats take over temporarily. These emotional indulgences create guilt, resentment, and competitiveness within the family group. Whenever I observe this sort of scene in a home, I feel a subtle temptation to tape the session and play it later when everyone is quiet and objective. When we react to adolescent emotionalism with a similar response, we are not helping a young person reach the goal of emotional maturity.

His feelings of embarrassment and defeat over his inability to control his emotions are quite enough without a tirade from a hysterical or self-pitying parent. "In quietness and in confidence shall be your strength" was the Scripture verse impressed upon me during some of the stormy sessions of my children's adolescence.[1] A parent, I found, can win more battles by knowing when to be quiet than by an avalanche of poorly timed words. Emotional control is not easy in adolescence and can be even harder when an overwrought parent gets into the act.

THE GOAL OF MARITAL MATURITY

The conflict over identification with one's own sex, which is present at ages four and five, seems to disappear at about six. It may not have been fully resolved, but the struggle for sex identity is postponed for later consideration while the competitive activities of middle childhood take over the focus of interest. When a child reaches the teens, this sex conflict is revived in preparation for mate choice and marriage. If there has been difficulty in the relationship with the parent of the opposite sex at four or five, the conflict will return at adolescence.

Until a young person has solved the problem of his sex identification, he is not ready to marry. Often very romantic attachments for friends of the same sex develop during early teens—jealous possessive liaisons which delay the need to take the leap into love relationships with the opposite sex. Sometimes adolescents even at sixteen or seventeen are torn between a sentimental relationship with a friend of the same sex and an attraction for a person of the opposite sex. This is not to be interpreted as a homosexual trend but only as a phase in the struggle to heterosexuality. The next phase may be a romantic idolization of an older person of the opposite sex. Usually the object of this "crush" is a popular personality, an entertainer, teacher, or perhaps a youth leader in the church. It is a perfectly harmless infatuation as long as the adult recipient of the admiration does not respond with seductiveness, thus exploiting the teenager's trustful adoration.

During teen years there may be some disruption in a child's home relationships, for teenagers sometimes feel a need to break their infantile emotional attachment to their parents. They may become overly critical of the parent of the opposite sex in preparation for a marital relationship. An adolescent may seem also to belittle his parent of the same sex, perhaps because he feels inadequate when he compares himself with his model of manhood or womanhood. Immature parents who have never really solved these conflicts in their own lives will be very threatened by their child's sudden change of attitude toward them.

To help a young person attain his identity as a male or a female it is important that the relationship of the parents be harmonious and satisfying. If the needs of one of the parents are not being met by the spouse there may be a reluctance to allow a teenager his emotional freedom. Sometimes it is necessary for a young person to leave home to gain his freedom from the excessive emotional attachment of such a parent. Until this freedom is attained a young person cannot form a happy marital relationship in which his mate will have first place in his loyalties and affections. If he enters marriage before he is mature in this sense, he will constantly invite parental interference in the marriage and will feel guilty about having deserted the parent with whom he has an infantile amorous attachment.

No wonder the Scriptures warn in three different places that a man shall leave his father and his mother, and shall cleave unto his wife.[2] This does not conflict with the command "Honour thy father and thy mother."[3] One command is talking about the matter of giving oneself to a mate as the person deserving priority over all others. The other is talking about giving love and respect to one's parents and does not condone the crippling neurotic attachment which some adults have for their parents. When parents free their children to form romantic attachments with friends of the opposite sex, they are making an investment in their future marital happiness.

THE GOAL OF ECONOMIC MATURITY

Of quite a different nature is the adolescent goal of economic maturity. In our society of easy credit and materialistic emphasis, it is doubly important that a young person be helped to attain economic maturity. Immaturity is often expressed by an inability to wait for the satisfaction of one's needs. Nothing spells failure more clearly than the excessive use of credit fostered by a tendency to seek immediate gratification of one's desires.

Teaching children to always expect immediate gratification for their desires is preparing them for economic immaturity. It is a wise parent who helps his young person learn not to sacrifice his future on the altar of the present. A teenager should have an adequate allowance and know what expenses he is responsible for. Instead of being underwritten if he does not handle his money wisely, he should take the consequences of his foolish spending. Young men who have never learned to restrict their spending become irresponsible husbands who are likely to squander their income on personal luxuries while neglecting basic family needs. Girls from the same homes are likely to have trouble living within their husband's income.

Parents need to teach their teens the pitfalls of excessive credit costs and the value of saving a portion of one's income. They should also be an example of a set of values which do not place "things" in top priority. The Bible warns against such attitudes when it urges that we not be "a lover of money—insatiable for wealth and ready to obtain it by questionable means."[4] It warns that "those who crave to be rich fall into temptation and a snare, and into many foolish (useless, godless) and hurtful desires that plunge men into ruin and destruction and miserable perishing. For the love of money is a root of all evils; it is through this craving that some have been led astray, and have wandered from the faith and pierced themselves through with many acute [mental] pangs."[5] Those who have failed to control their cravings and have fallen into the habit of excessive use of credit will readily understand the "acute mental pangs" of the debtor.

24

Are There More Goals of Growing Up?

THERE ARE OTHER GOALS OF maturity—some very important ones follow.

THE GOAL OF MORAL MATURITY

In earlier generations it seemed easier than it is now for a young person to reach moral maturity. The home, the school and the church were all fairly consistent in their teachings about moral standards, but today there is a confusing inconsistency. In the same newspaper a youth can read an article written by a clergyman which states that the moral principles of the Ten Commandments are not valid for modern society, and a column which attacks premarital sex. In the same school a pupil may have one teacher whom he knows to be a Christian with high moral standards, and another teacher who comes in on Monday morning suffering from a hangover and whose health lectures make it quite clear that indulgence in premarital sex is neither right nor wrong but just a matter of personal taste.

No wonder young people are adrift on a sea of moral insecurity. They may feel pressured by friends into acting in a manner which is contrary to their own conscience.

Moral maturity involves the establishing of a set of standards by which one lives, and these standards cannot be decided in the heat of a moment of sexual excitement. Nor should they be decided on the basis of whether one really loves the person who is inviting him to enjoy sexual relations. I remember one young man who, in trying to fly by these modern signals, had sexual relations with three girls within six months because each time he thought he was genuinely in love. Each time his infatuation died out shortly after sexual relations. Each time a girl's trust in men was blasted.

Another young man said he believed that it was quite all right to satisfy sexual hungers in the same way that one satisfies the desire for food—anytime and with anyone he wished. Later he confided that he had fallen in love with a girl whom he wanted to marry but he couldn't seem to make a final decision because she was the mother of an infant child born out of wedlock. I began to explore his reluctance—whether it was to take on the extra financial responsibility or whether he had difficulty in accepting the father role.

Finally he blurted out with obvious embarrassment that he just did not like to face the fact that another man had been allowed sexual intimacies with the woman he now loved. I asked him if he felt his future wife would feel the same way if she knew about all of his sexual adventures. He thought she would. Although rationally he had accepted the standards of sexual permissiveness, emotionally he had not. Unknown premarital sexual partners had come like intruders to haunt the marital relationship. This is not uncommon. The Christian view insists that a person should not have the privileges of sexual intimacy until he is ready to make a public commitment to the person he loves in a legal marriage.

Therefore, it is urgent that young people establish their own moral code and be true to these standards. The Bible calls adultery and fornication sin. Stealing, lying and covetousness are all morally wrong according to divine standards. In many circles, petty thievery is a clever joke, lying is a method of getting along in the world without becoming unpopular, adultery is getting rid of "harmful" sexual tensions, and covetousness is admirable "go ahead." Bible-based virtues may not be popular but they build a society in which there are trust and respect—sound foundations for good relationships. A young person would do well to consider the Christian standards before establishing his own personal moral code.

God is the absolute standard of righteousness, and an intimate relationship with Him touches every area of our behavior. Our own standards are not absolutely right. At best we have a hazy view of righteousness, but we who are Christians know that there is an absolute in God. The opinion of the majority in any given society is not the source of the Christian's moral code, for the fact that "everybody is doing it" means nothing to a Christian's view of right and wrong. To him, this is like judging physical health standards by the health of the culture in which one lives. By this criteria people in hungry Biafra should be content with just enough strength to walk around.

No young person has come to moral maturity until he has decided for himself what his moral standards will be.

The Goal of Vocational Maturity

Before the end of the adolescent period, which most believe extends from age thirteen to twenty-five, a young person has usually established vocational goals or has already entered his vocation. How often adolescents have been confused and hindered in this decision by pressure from a parent to follow a certain favored vocation. Sometimes there are parental prejudices against service vocations or trades. Other parents who are in trades themselves are threatened by a son who wants to continue his schooling and enter one of the professions. The Talmud wisely says, "Limit not thy children to thine own desires. They are born in a different time."

Young people from church homes tell me that sometimes they feel they have disappointed their parents by not choosing full-time Christian service as a vocation. I am quick to tell them that all work is full-time Christian service if one views his work as a service to God. It seems unfair that the church often gives great recognition to those who decide to become ministers or missionaries, while making those who are called to become doctors, teachers or carpenters feel like second-rate Christians. This puts young people under pressure in their vocational choices and also encourages entrance into the ministry by individuals who do not belong there.

We should give as much encouragement to a God-motivated teacher as to a candidate for the ministry. The criteria for Christian service is not what kind of a job one does but whether or not an individual is serving God in the vocation which, after prayerful consideration, he feels he should choose.

Christianity is a way of life which needs to infiltrate every area and level of contemporary society. In this sense, whether one writes, doctors, builds, sells, or types, he is a representative for God; and one of the best influences we can offer for Christ is the quality of our work.

Young people have not reached vocational maturity until they have the self-knowledge and healthy motivations to choose a suitable vocation, and the willingness to invest the time and energy involved in thorough preparation for and efficient execution of their work. This is one of the goals of adolescence which requires much thought and self-searching on the part of young people, and much understanding and tolerance on the part of parents. Vocational testing is sometimes helpful in the choice, but it is a personal decision which must not be interfered with and it may involve several unsatisfactory choices before the final choice is made.

The Goal of Spiritual Maturity

Social maturity involves, among other things, moving from complete dependence upon one's parents to independence. Spiritual maturity involves moving from dependence on oneself or others to full dependence upon God. Some people rebel against this idea because they are reluctant to admit that they need any kind of dependence. When human beings deny their need for the one who is Creator and Sustainer of all things, it is like a rugged oak outgrowing its need for the earth in which it is rooted. When a tree—even a strong one—rejects the soil in which it grew, it soon shrivels and dies. So it is with the individual who thinks he has outgrown his need for God.

The Bible describes what dependence on God involves: "Trust in the LORD with all thine heart; and lean not unto thine own understanding. In all thy ways acknowledge him, and he shall direct thy paths."[1]

Spirituality is not having a "quiet time," or witnessing, or attending church or "saying grace" at meals. A person can do all of these things and be a proud, cantankerous, self-willed snob in his attitude to God and his fellowmen. Spirituality is not conforming to the world that Christians have woven around themselves like caterpillars in a cocoon.

Spiritual maturity is placing full dependence on God. It is what Moses did when he looked an alluring future straight in the face and then "chose rather" to follow God and His plan.[2] This is dependence on God—fully trusting His love, wisdom, strength and guidance. This is the essence of spiritual maturity —happy is the young person who finds it early in life.

Parents can help most by knowing this dependence themselves. Young people may enter adulthood before reaching all of these goals, but the fact that they have goals will still be to their advantage. Like Paul, they will continue to "press on toward the . . . prize to which God in Christ Jesus is calling . . . [them] upward."[3] These adolescent goals are important and many of them should continue as life goals long after adolescence.

Part VI

YOU AND YOUR PARENTAL
FAMILY RELATIONSHIPS

25

Life's Most Significant Influence— The Mother Relationship

TO TRY TO DESCRIBE the influence of a mother in the life of her child would be to invite failure. That is why I prefer to have you experience what a mother relationship has meant in my own life.

I don't remember whether the long ribbed stockings which I wore as a child were always mended or not. I can't even recall how well my mother kept house. There are, however, some memories which make her my life's most unforgettable character.

Mother spent few days in high school, for my grandmother died when she was ten, leaving her the oldest of six children. But God gave her a hungry mind which went on satisfying itself throughout life so that her lack of schooling never showed.

As a scrawny kid I was exposed to many of the literary greats. How well I remember the howl of the wind in the stovepipes and the smell of warm paint from the hot pipes as we sat around the coal stove during long winter evenings. Light from the red coals flickered through the mica windows of the stove, casting shadows across my mother's face as she read aloud to us from the classics. Every mood was expressed on her face as we traveled through the trials and triumphs of Tiny Tim or Nicholas Nickleby. Sometimes the soft drone of her voice would stop and her tears would flow till my father would take up the reading in his jerking gait. He was more equipped for hammer and nails than for the classics, but there he was one with us. Mother loved poetry too. John Milton's *Paradise Lost* was read to us long before we could comprehend its full meaning. Though the sense of the words sometimes passed us by, their music became a part of us. The King James Version of the Bible had its place in our home too. It was read aloud more and more as the years went by and the heartaches of the great depression rolled in upon us.

First my father's business went, then our home, but Mother kept on at her job with apparent disregard for trouble. I can still remember trudging home from high school in hand-me-down clothes and hearing Mother's shrill soprano warbling through the intricacies of the "Hallelujah Chorus." All she lacked to make her a truly great singer was a pretty voice. She settled for a place in the church choir and learned whole sections of the great oratorios by memory.

This passion for music implanted the same hunger in her children. We carted home every castoff instrument we could find and, armed with instruction books from Woolworths, we tried to play them. Our neighbors suffered the chaos of guitar-strumming, horn-blowing and piano-thumping successively for years.

I well remember the night my musical efforts nearly set the house on fire. I was experimenting with a trombone—loaned by the school band. Not having the luxury of a music stand, I propped my music on the bookcase beside a kerosene lamp—at that moment our electricity was off because there was no money to pay the bill. I became so intent on producing a sound, which teetered between a groan and a burp, that I pushed the slide out and sent the lamp crashing to the floor. All of this never discouraged Mother. She was so happy to see that her love of music was being reproduced in her children that no inconvenience mattered. She began fabric-painting to provide us with piano lessons at fifty cents an hour. It seemed that she could do anything she turned her hand to. If there was a verse to be written, a picture to be painted, a speech to be given or bread to be baked, she could do it all equally well.

Sometimes visitors to our home—and there were many—

would become aware of her varied talents and turn to my father and say, "Do you sing or paint, Mr. McKay?"

He would smile in his quiet Scottish way and, while he was still deciding how to answer, Mother would come to his rescue.

"Dad is an artist in wood," she would say admiringly. "He builds beautiful homes. He is a genius at figuring things out too." Then she would go on with a much-told story to illustrate his superior ability.

"You know," she would say, "I once tried to make a velvet suit for my boy. Patterns are just impossible for me to fathom, and I'm not too domesticated anyway. Well, I gave up in tears. When Dad came home from work, he found me crying over a chaos of royal blue velvet. 'Never mind,' he said, 'Leave it till tomorrow. You'll get it then.' After supper he sent me smiling off to choir practice. Well, when I got home he had the whole thing put together, ready for sewing. He figured it all out from the pattern."

She never divulged that Dad sang in the most horrible monotone I have ever heard. Or that we kids would get great sport from playing a note on the piano and laughing at his good-natured attempts to sing it. To hear her talk, people would think her a helpless creature and Dad the stability of the family.

There were other stories she shrewdly used to create this illusion. One of her favorites was the story of her attempt to fill a fountain pen—an old-fashioned type—with a rubber tube which filled by removing it from the barrel and depressing it by hand. She would laugh gaily as she told how she filled the tube and then placed it between her teeth—nib in—while she covered the ink bottle. When she took the pen out of her mouth she snatched it by the tube and squirted a stream of ink into her mouth.

By the time she finished, the guests were pitying my father for having to live with such a stupid woman. An awkward situation was bridged, and everyone was in a rollicking mood. But we all knew that Mother was not stupid; she was smart enough to outwit the depression's defeating effects.

Finally the "lean years" passed and we gathered up what little remained and moved to a rented house. Three months later the 1937 Ontario flood swept in upon us and ruined most of what we had salvaged from the depression. Mother's many friends, knowing her already difficult path, came to sympathize but found her radiant.

"You know," she told them, "the night before the flood I awoke with a verse from the Bible running through my mind: 'For the LORD God is a sun and shield: the LORD will give grace and glory: no good thing will he withhold from them that walk uprightly.' How can I complain with a promise like that?" she asked.

But there was one more trial ahead. In 1940 Mother developed cancer. She spent the next year dying, pound by pound. When she knew what was ahead of her she wrote the following lines:

> Storm clouds may gather far out on the skyline,
>   Fierce the temptations marking my way.
> I have a risen conquering Saviour,
>   Giving abundantly, strength for the day.
>
> Songs of deliverance, praises ascending,
>   Out of deep grief and trials are born.
> What though the night hangs low on my pathway,
>   Yonder there breaks the light of the morn.
>
> Conquering faith, in conflict and battle,
>   Joy, when the clouds of sorrow abound.
> Heaven at last with Him in the Glory,
>   All that I need in my Saviour I've found.

Then one Saturday in February, 1941, at high noon, she slipped away to be with the one who had piloted her life's ship through many storms. For two days people filed in and out past her casket. Some of these people I could not even remember meeting before.

"Your mother stayed with me when my baby died," one said.

"I shall never forget what your mother meant to me when my boy got into court," another confided.

"Your mother opened her home to me when I was a penniless immigrant," said a young Irishman with tears in his eyes. "She mended my clothes and cheered many lonely hours till I earned enough to bring my wife and family to Canada."

"Your mother was our adopted mother when we were off duty with nowhere to go," said a group of student nurses.

So it went for two days until we were weary with listening.

No wonder we used the words of the great apostle Paul as our tribute to her: "We give thanks to God always for you, . . . remembering without ceasing your work of faith, and labour of love, and patience of hope in our Lord Jesus Christ."[1]

Mother, I know now, was the most significant influence of my life—the social foundation upon which all other relationships have been built.

26

Can You Help Me Understand My Parents?

THE FAMILY is the earliest and most significant influence an individual will ever experience. In today's world there is concern among many over the deterioration of family life. In our mobile society the family hearth is largely deserted, and often two people living under the same roof seldom cross paths. Unfortunately the church has made its contribution to this situation by multiplying its activities.

It is very easy under such (often unavoidable) circumstances for members of a family to grow apart and have little influence on each other. Another factor that has negated family influence is the modern tendency to discount the experiences and insights of the past, which are sometimes written off as neither valuable nor relevant to the present generation. This attitude is the result of pragmatic thought and its emphasis on the here and now.

YOU AND YOUR PARENTS

When I was a child every fifth-grade pupil in my home city received a copy of the book of Proverbs. I remember how impressed I was with some of the wisdom contained in the book. I especially noticed the strong emphasis on the value of parental instruction. When comparing those verses with the present-day situation, I feel that we must either change some of our ideas about the role of parents or write a new version of the book of Proverbs. The following rendition, though exaggerated for emphasis, is my attempt to update Proverbs to the thinking of our space age:

PROVERBS FOR THE SPACE AGE

My son, let me give thee some tips for successful living. A wise man will hear everyone, giving each man's opinion equal value, whether his ideas have worked in his own life or not. One thing remember, yea two, let not thyself be too much influenced by the instruction of thy father and be not afraid to go against the law of thy mother. For behold, we know in this age of experimentalism that antiquity hath no ideas relevant to our changing social milieu.

Therefore, my son, gird up thy loins for adventure and open thy heart to new ideas; be not fearful of consequences. Whether thine actions bring ill consequences or happy results, be not afraid, for how canst thy learning be complete without experience and thy philosophy relevant without trial and error. Give thyself, therefore, to the experiences of today without regard to the rules of yesterday or the results of tomorrow. Have you not heard that success in modern living demands appropriate responses to present situations? Therefore, my son, away with old standards—live in a brave new world. Learn, my son, to interpret situations individually and come up with appropriate behavior—tailor-made for the occasion. Otherwise, thou shalt, all thy lifetime, be in bondage to taboos forced upon thee by thine elders, many of whom are still willing captives of the establishment.

Beware of authority, my son, and refrain thy feet from its path. How shall change be made in the establishment if thou dost accept the authority of its institutions? Therefore, revolt thou against this evil. By sit-ins and marches refuse thou to cooperate until thou hast a controlling voice in institutional affairs.

If all of this freedom and independence disturbs thy security, think it not strange, for thou art pioneering a new morality. In due season, when the transition is complete, security will return to thy heart. Until then, be brave; we have discovered many chemical comforts to help thee. Take care that thou use them wisely and beware of the police. These diehards of the establishment may distress thee sore and interfere with thy freedoms.

One more warning, my son, beware of work. It is a Puritan ethic which may keep thee from fulfilling thyself. What do material things matter anyway? Why earn thy paycheck in drudgery! Draw aside, meditate, love, find answers to life! Take no notice of the ant, thou thinker! He is busy storing up for tomorrow, and ye are but interested in today. Sponge thy food and clothing and spend thy time thinking, and in due season thou shalt have answers, while the ants of society will have paid all their substance in taxes to keep thee and thy friends.

Now about love, that blessed quality of closeness. Run thou after it diligently and thou shalt find it. Thy parents never knew true love. Here is thy challenge to seek new frontiers. Love, and thy world will love with thee. Not with that sullied kind of devotion which causes a man to go through "blood, sweat and tears" for his country, in order to preserve liberty and bring safety to friend and family, nor that tinsel variety of love which is expressed in terms of food for hungry little mouths, and shoes for little bare feet, and music lessons, and cub packs and hockey teams. This is the materialistic kind of love which thy parents in their ignorance gave unto thee. Because of its inadequacy it hath drawn thee to drugs, and long hair and filthy garments. Forgive our shortcomings and discover thou a new variety of love, more adequate and effective than that of thine elders. Find thou love which elevates to nobler deeds, like passing flowers to strangers and sacrificing sleep to commune with friends that pass in the night. Take no thought if thou be too tired to rise up in the morning and earn thy bread, for love is more important.

Forgive me, son, none of this should I have written thee. I have tried to give thee past wisdom in line with thy brave new world. Alas, for I have erred. I should not have hindered thee even with my revised opinions. My hangup for the old ways still lingers. All wrong have I been! Forgive thou me! And to think that I began my interference so early in thy young life, teaching you to walk! And then to run to the gate when I came home from work. Go to now! Forget my admonitions unto thee. Go unfettered by conventions. Go to! And may thine own works praise thee in the gates.

"Ridiculous," you say. Then perhaps we should leave the proverbs as they have always been and change our attitudes instead.

Sometimes young people feel that their parents are wrong about certain things—and they can be wrong. Regardless of this possibility, it is wise, until a child is self-supporting at least, for that child to submit himself to his own parents. If, after all attempts to discuss some matter in question with his parents, he has failed to change their opinion, he should accept their decision and abide by it, whether he thinks it is right or wrong. For two reasons—one, because they are older and more experienced and therefore are often right in the long run. Second, even if they are wrong, they are his parents and have the position of authority in their own home; and he has both a moral obligation and a social responsibility to accept that authority respectfully and humbly. This is the reason the Bible repeats over and over the command to children to obey their parents and to honor their father and mother.[1] God gave to parents the responsibility for the behavior of their children, and He expects children to respond humbly to this God-given authority. Someday those same children will have children of their own and can command their household. The Bible says, "A wise son maketh a glad father."[2] A son who has learned to accept parental authority will not abuse it when he has that authority himself.

JESUS AND HIS PARENTS

Jesus, the Son of God, was without human flaw. His mother and foster-father were human and therefore mistaken sometimes in their judgment. If any child deserved the right to disobey his parents, Jesus did. Yet the Bible states that after His visit to the temple in Jerusalem, where He talked with the doctors at the age of twelve, "he went down with them [his parents], and came to Nazareth, and was subject unto them."[3] If divine wisdom was humble enough to be subject to human frailty, why should Christian young people refuse to obey their parents?

When Jesus grew to adulthood, however, His obligation to obey His parents ended. At the marriage of Cana He courteously made it clear to His mother that she no longer had a right to command His personal decisions. Parental control need not be accepted by grown and self-supporting young people, either married or single, in making their life decisions. However, respect and courtesy are always in order, and the humility to request and consider the opinions of a parent before making a decision is helpful.

If grown children are living under the parental roof, while they are not obligated to allow their parents to make their personal decisions, they do have an obligation to cooperate in the family organization. This includes such courtesies as notifying

their mother when they expect to be absent for a meal or overnight, and being thoughtful and helpful around the home. A
young person should pay board to the support of the home as
soon as he is steadily employed. Any other arrangement encourages dependency.

The road to maturity runs from complete dependence at infancy, through ever increasing independence in childhood, and
ends in complete independence by the end of adolescence. This
process requires much wisdom and self-control on the part of
parents and a spirit of growing self-sufficiency on the part of
children. For a parent to move from the place of complete control over his child to a place of complete abdication from that
control requires both sensitivity and emotional maturity.

"I GET ALONG WITH MOTHER BUT DAD IS TOO STRICT"

Many, especially in our society of confused sex identification,
are not aware of the importance of the father's place in the
home. Father love is different from mother love, and both are
important in the healthy development of a child. Fromm in his
book *The Art of Loving* has much to say on this subject. He
states,

> Motherly love by its very nature is unconditional; mother loves
> the newborn infant because it is her child, not because the child
> has fulfilled any specific conditions, or lived up to any specific ex-
> pectation. . . . The relationship to father is quite different,
> mother is the home we come from, she is nature, soil . . . father
> does not represent any such natural home. He has little connection
> with the child in the first years of its life, and his importance for
> the child in this early period cannot be compared with that of
> mother. While father does not represent the natural world, he
> represents the other pole of human existence; the world of
> thought, of man made things, of law and order, of discipline, of
> travel and adventure. Father is the one who teaches the child, who
> shows him the road into the world. . . .
>
> Fatherly love is conditional love. Its principle is "I love you
> because you do your duty, because you are like me. . . ." Fatherly
> love has to be deserved. . . . In the nature of fatherly love lies the
> fact that obedience becomes the main virtue and disobedience the
> main sin. . . . Since fatherly love is conditioned, I can do some-

thing to acquire it . . . his love is not outside my control as unconditional mother love is. . . . The infant needs unconditional love
and care psychologically as well as physically; the child, especially
after six also needs father's love, his authority and guidance.
Mother has the function of making him secure in life, father has
the function of teaching him, guiding him to cope with those
problems with which the particular society the child has been
born into confronts him.[4]

This quotation is impressive, coming from one of the world's
best-known living psychoanalysts whose book on love has sold
200,000 copies in hard cover, not to mention its wide sale in
paperback editions.

Long before Fromm, the Bible placed the responsibility of
training and teaching children upon the father.[5] It comments
that "a wise son heareth his father's instruction."[6]

In our generation both mothers and children have failed to
accept this role of the father. Mothers have been guilty of
judging their husbands as too strict because they are not aware
of these two kinds of love, each so necessary to a child's development. How often I have found it necessary to point out and
explain this difference to young men and their protective mothers. These youths would not be delinquent if their mothers
had allowed their fathers to exercise their authority in the home.
Mother love has covered for her boys, protecting them against
father's more demanding kind of love. One of the roles of a
faithful father is to protect his children, especially his sons, from
the overprotection of their mother. His influence will aid children in learning how to meet the expectations of society.

Young people who have a father who knows how to say "no"
effectively have a great asset. Both mothers and children should
appreciate such a man's influence in the home, even though at
times his requirements may seem strict by their standards. If a
child has the understanding love of a mother to give him security and acceptance, and the more demanding love of a father
to discipline him to right behavior, he has a great heritage. No
wonder the Bible says, "Train up a child in the way he should
go: and when he is old, he will not depart from it."[7]

27

Brothers! Sisters! Grandparents! What About Them?

MOST YOUNG PEOPLE have other members in their families besides parents. Sometimes fierce rivalry develops in these relationships; at other times, deep love and loyalty characterize these attachments.

YOU AND YOUR BROTHERS AND SISTERS

Many examples of brother relationships are in literature. Some of the best known are in the Bible. Some are creative and meaningful, others are destructive and envious. Sometimes a person's whole life is affected by a poor brother or sister relationship. Jealousy is common between children of the same parents, and is often fostered by parental favoritism as in the case of Jacob and Esau, and Joseph and his brothers. Earth's first murder was committed because of sibling rivalry, jealousy between children of the same parents.

It is sad when individuals fail to overcome their infantile feelings of resentment at the arrival of a new baby. It is said that all of us have at some time wished to be only children. I have talked with adults who still carried deep bitterness against a brother or sister and who later vented these feelings on a daughter or son. Their child then became the victim of earlier feelings of resentment. Such unfair and unexplainable rejection can cause antisocial tendencies in a child which can affect his whole life. The parent cannot himself explain why he constantly belittles and criticizes this particular child.

Usually, however, a brother or sister "is born for adversity," as the Bible states.[1] Brothers and sisters share common family sorrows and joys. They stand together at the same nursery windows, the same open graves, and the same bridal altars. As the years pass, the comradeship of the playroom develops into the concerned interest of adulthood. Members of families often travel many miles to be with each other in times of adversity. Though time and distance seem to part brothers and sisters, and new family ties occupy their attention, the comradeship of the playroom never quite dies in a good brother or sister relationship.

It is fitting to note in Scripture that the reflective, stable Andrew brought his more excitable and extroverted brother, Peter, to Jesus. He knew both Peter's needs and his own. It is refreshing also to observe Esau, the rough out-of-doors man, forgiving his mother's spoiled baby, Jacob. Esau's tears that day washed away the resentment and fear that had clouded their love for sixty-five years.

There may be modern Esaus and Jacobs whose whole lives have been blighted by envy and hatred against each other. These would do well to follow the example of Esau's forgiveness. The Bible warns against such feelings and their effect on others when it says, "Look diligently lest any man fail of the grace of God; lest any root of bitterness springing up trouble you, and thereby many be defiled."[2]

YOU AND YOUR GRANDPARENTS

Perhaps in your home you have grown up with grandparents under the same roof. No grandparent should usurp a parent's right to raise his own children, and a young person would be wise not to use a grandparent's interference to get his own way. When people are older they are far too permissive to raise children, although it is sometimes necessary because of death or separation.

However, nearby grandparents can have a great influence on a child because of their greater availability. Paul told Timothy that he had "sincere and unqualified faith [the leaning of your entire personality on God in Christ in absolute trust and con-

fidence in His power, wisdom and goodness, a faith] that first
lived permanently in (the heart of) your grandmother Lois and
your mother Eunice and now, I [Paul] am [fully] persuaded,
(dwells) in you [Timothy] also."[3] Paul seems here to intimate
that not only the influence of a Christian mother, but the influence of his Christian grandmother touched Timothy's life.
Grandmother can be quite a significant person in the life of a
child. An eight-year-old in third grade tells why in the following description:

WHAT IS A GRANDMA?

A grandmother is a lady who has no children of her own,
so she likes other people's little girls. A grandfather is
a man grandmother. He goes for walks with the boys,
and they talk fishing and things like that.

Grandmas don't have anything to do except be there.
It is enough if they drive us to the supermarket where
the pretend horse is and have lots of dimes ready. Or
if they take us for walks, they should slow down past
pretty leaves and caterpillars. They should never say
"Hurry up."

Usually they are fat, but not too fat to tie kids shoes.
They wear glasses and funny underwear. They can take
their teeth and gums off.

They don't have to be smart, only answer questions like
why dogs hate cats and how come God isn't married?
They don't talk visitors' talk like visitors do, because it
is hard to understand.

When they read to us they don't skip words or mind if
it is the same story again. Everybody should try to have
a grandmother, especially if you don't have television
because grandmas are the only grownups who have got
time.

These are the secondary family relationships that so greatly
influence our early life. These and many others—uncles, aunts
and cousins—help us form habits and values. They give us
our early lessons about life and people.

Part VII

YOU AND OTHER RELATIONSHIPS

28

Are My Friends Really That Important?

TENNYSON SAID in his *Ulysses,* "I am part of all that I have met." This is especially true of our friends.

YOU AND YOUR FRIENDS

In earlier societies, friendship seemed to have a much larger place than in ours. People had time to communicate on a deep level, and friendship played a large part in their lives. Happy is the man in our society who has a close friend. Often a heavy burden can be lightened or a difficult problem solved by talking it out with another man. Strength and courage are transmitted in male relationships which a husband cannot always receive in discussing certain problems with his wife.

Conversely, most women need female friends to find the sensitivity and understanding which only another woman can give in certain situations. The female characteristic of tenderness—the heritage of women which prepares them for motherhood—is appreciated by most adults. Men usually find this quality in their wives, while women often need to seek it in friendships with other women.

I recall the discouragement of a young woman who was in charge of sports at one of the women's retreats where I spoke. She was blaming her program for the women's indifference to these recreational activities. This amused me greatly for I have never yet observed an enthusiastic sports program at such a gathering. When women get together they enjoy talking about their common problems and experiences. Other activities become secondary.

Women in our society are very lonely, for they do not have

the opportunity for friendship which women in more primitive societies have. Even in our pioneer days, women met together for quilting bees. While their needles were flying, so were their tongues, and many deep lessons in family living were communicated on these occasions. Often I have been told by women on probation that they appreciate having another woman to share their problems. Previously they were carrying their burdens alone. We all need friends as well as family.

Friendship is described beautifully in the Bible account of David and Jonathan: "The soul of Jonathan was knit with the soul of David, and Jonathan loved him as his own soul."[1] Because of this, Jonathan saved David from his father's murderous intentions, at the risk of his own life. Yet, a friend who is described as one who "loveth at all times," can also wound.[2] "Faithful are the wounds of a friend."[3] There is no better way to come to self-awareness than to share a deep and lasting friendship. "Iron sharpeneth iron; so a man sharpeneth the countenance of his friend," the Bible declares.[4]

A nineteenth-century poetess puts it this way:

FRIENDSHIP

Oh the comfort—the inexpressible comfort of
   feeling safe with a person
Having neither to weigh thoughts,
Nor measure words—but pouring them
All right out—just as they are—
Chaff and grain together—
Certain that a faithful hand will
Take and sift them—
Keeping what is worth keeping—
And with the breath of kindness
Blow the rest away.

                DINAH MARIE MULOCK (CRAIK)

This is true friendship. Unfortunately some people pervert so-called friendship into a kindly (later not so kindly) domination. This kind of attachment is a greedy swallowing up of another love-hungry individual. The only illustration I can give to describe such an obsession is the attachment of Siamese twins. They are certainly never lonely, but they must often crave privacy and independent action. This pseudo-friendship admits no other relationship and discourages personal growth in both individuals. At first it is filled with glamour and excitement, but as time goes on, the restricting nature of the relationship develops deep conflicts. That is, unless one of the friends denies his selfhood completely. Even then the obsession fades because the domineering member of the relationship no longer has a challenge and leaves for greater conquests. The dominated person then feels more lonely than ever before and is left drained, like a wilted plant, of every ounce of confident selfhood.

I have seen these "friendships" drag normally law-abiding people into crime, robbing them of the motivation to care what happens in their future. When the whole world collapses at the end of such an emotional attachment, they are open invitations to a new domination.

Fromm in *The Art of Loving* calls this a "symbiotic union."[5] It has its biological pattern, he notes, in the relationship between a pregnant mother and her unborn child. Mother and child live together and the fully dependent child receives everything it needs from its mother. This is a good picture of a symbiotic relationship which grows out of extreme longings for dependency coupled with extreme desire for domination. Such a "friendship" hardly deserves the name since it is so binding and damaging that it hinders both the psychological birth and growth of the individual.

I have observed both the exhilaration and the deep conflicts of such dependency relationships. Sometimes sexual feelings enter, giving the relationship homosexual overtones.

Young people and adults alike can change the course of their lives by their choice of friends. A good choice can mean that we are inspired to higher living, while a poor choice may drag us down to ignoble deeds and unhealthy attitudes. Delinquent young people seem to have difficulty distinguishing between their friends and their enemies.

True friendship is the emotional and intellectual sharing of two independent and autonomous individuals. It is not threatened by other relationships and can survive the strains of separation and the passing of years. When real friends meet after long separation they still feel the closeness that David and Jonathan felt when their souls were "knit together." There is no substitute for this kind of friendship.

29

How Can I Learn to Handle My Authority Relationships?

SOME INDIVIDUALS seem to find difficulty in every relationship with an authority figure—the boss, the teacher, and civil authorities. Often this problem begins in childhood when they experience a poor relationship with a parent who misuses his or her authority to deprive a child of his rights. The hostility engendered then is transferred to every other authority relationship.

YOU AND YOUR EMPLOYER-EMPLOYEE RELATIONSHIPS

The Bible has a number of things to say to employers and employees. Once again in this area, society has moved away from the scriptural view of relationships. The modern problem of the excessive demands of labor which are crippling today's economy is the result of the kind of management which has been more concerned about profit than about people. Perhaps as a reaction to this, there is little concern on the part of employees for the quality and quantity of work which they offer for a full day's pay.

Paul urges the Christians to "apply themselves to honorable occupations."[1] He said, "Be obedient to those who are your physical masters, having respect for them and eager concern to please them, in singleness of motive and with all your heart, as [service] to Christ [Himself]. Not in the way of eyeservice—as if they were watching you—and only to please men; but as servants (slaves) of Christ, doing the will of God heartily and with your whole soul; rendering service readily with goodwill,

179

as to the Lord and not to men."[2] He also tells employees not "to steal by taking things of small value, but to prove themselves truly loyal and entirely reliable and faithful throughout, so that in everything they may be an ornament and do credit to the teaching [which is from and about] God our Savior."[3] Apparently employees had the same temptations in that day as in ours.

Again Peter admonishes household servants to "be submissive to your masters with all (proper) respect, not only to those who are kind, considerate and reasonable but also to those who are surly—overbearing, unjust and crooked."[4]

That would be unfair if Paul did not also tell employers to act on the same principle of pleasing God in their treatment of others. He urges, "You masters, act on the same [principle] toward them [those who serve you], and give up threatening and using violent and abusive words, knowing that He Who is both their Master and yours is in heaven, and there is no respect of persons—no partiality—with Him."[5]

The Old Testament warns employers: "Thou shalt not defraud thy neighbour, neither rob him: the wages of him that is hired shall not abide with thee all night until the morning."[6] This command was given to a society which paid wages by the day. The employer's attitude is also censored, "Thou shalt not rule over him with rigour; but shalt fear thy God."[7] In another place employers are urged not to take advantage of an immigrant, oppressing him as a hired servant.[8]

Paul finally says bluntly, "Masters, give unto your servants that which is just and equal; knowing that ye also have a Master in heaven."[9] And "the labourer is worthy of his reward."[10]

James gives a scathing denunciation of stingy, exploitive employers when he cries out, "Behold, the hire of the labourers who have reaped down your fields, which is of you kept back by fraud, crieth: and the cries of them which have reaped are entered into the ears of the Lord."[11] "Look! The judge is [already] standing at the very door."[12] Apparently employers in Bible times had the same exploitive tendencies as in our day.

Today the worker with his unreasonable demands and organized power seems to be more of a threat to our security than exploitive employers. Jeremiah in the book of Lamentations expressed fear of this kind of domination in his sad day of anarchy and rebellion against authority: "Servants have ruled over us: there is none that doth deliver us out of their hand."[13]

Christianity has much to say to the present-day problem of employer-employee strife and unrest. Once again, Christian integrity in the hearts of workers and management would help solve the injustices and conflicts of both labor and capital.

YOUR STUDENT-TEACHER RELATIONSHIPS

Another area of serious difficulty in our society is that of student-teacher relationships. Student revolt is threatening our great schools, and possibly both students and schools have their own reasons for discontent with our present systems of education. In every generation there has been reaction on the part of idealistic youth against the staid traditionalism of adulthood. This is healthy; it is the source of social changes which take place from generation to generation. The leaders of each generation have been instigators of change in their university days. But today we see more than the reaction of youth against the conventions of age. We see, as always, youth needing to react and change society; but we see also a society which offers little stability against which to react.

Michael Demiashkevitch in his book *An Introduction to the Philosophy of Education* finds two complementary forces at work in society making sound progress possible.[14] The "mobility aspect" is seen in the clamor for social changes, and the "equilibrium aspect" is represented by the social institutions which conserve the past as an inheritance by which the present generation can profit. He proposes that the school in educating for social progress has the twofold task of giving expression to both these aspects. And he notes that the mobility aspect gets adequate expression from students—the voice of the new generation. The danger is that each new generation will not be sufficiently in

touch with the "equilibrium aspect" of social progress. The
school can help society keep its balance by placing its emphasis
on this aspect.

Demiashkevitch wrote his book in 1935 and possibly even
then saw the trend of education to give emphasis to the "mobility aspect." We are now reaping the results of the failure of
modern education to provide the stability against which youth
can safely react. Instead, education is inclined to ignore the rich
contributions from the racial fund of the past and to join youth
in its reaction against the stabilizing institutions of society.

The Bible has much to say to both revolting youth and to
modern educational institutions with their pragmatic emphasis
on the present and their rejection of past knowledge as being
irrelevant to the present. It indicates that the counsel of older
generations is to be valued by youth. Peter urges, "Likewise, ye
younger, submit yourselves unto the elder."[15] The wise man Solomon advises the young to apply their hearts unto instruction
and their ears unto the words of knowledge.[16] The two letters of
the aged Paul to young Timothy are an example of how the
counsel of a person of rich experience in life can be a strength
and guide to the young.

Bogoslavsky in his book *The Ideal School* indicates what he
considers to be the twofold objective of education. In terms of
knowledge, it is a total outlook; and in terms of the self, it is
the achievement of a superior life. He says the aim of education is "to help students to live rich and significant lives, to
build harmonious and colorful personalities, to enjoy to the ut-
most the glory of being happy, to face suffering when it comes
with dignity and profit, and finally to help other people to live
this superior life."[17] Another great educator defines education
as a mature person teaching the immature.

Young people in the educational setting of today need the
advice of James: "Let every man be swift to hear, slow to
speak."[18] The principal of a teacher's college in my city recently
asserted that our modern methods of education are producing
a generation of good talkers and poor listeners. A mother had

the right idea when she told her children that God gave them two ears and one mouth and He expected them to keep the balance between talking and listening that way. Little mention is made today about such attitudes as humility and respect, which should characterize the relationships of the young with older generations. Job observes that "with the ancient is wisdom; and in length of days understanding."[19] I have never met a truly learned person who did not exhibit a humble and teachable attitude toward all men, no matter how unlearned they might be.

David, perhaps the most creative personality of all the authors of Scripture, and Solomon, who was considered the wise man of his day, both repeat the premise that "the fear [reverential trust] of the LORD is the beginning of wisdom."[20] The founders of many of the early universities—Yale, Harvard, Princeton and Oxford—held the same view of the source of true knowledge.[21]

According to the mid-twentieth-century Harvard Report on Education under the title of "General Education in a Free Society," "Religion is *not* now for most colleges a practicable source of intellectual unity." The report indicates that we must search for a new source of unity for education, which presently lacks a unifying principle.[22] Walter Lippman, American journalist, wisely observed that "the more men have become separated from the spiritual heritage which binds them together, the more has education become egoist, careerist, specialist and asocial."[23] Timothy described the same flaw when he said that people in later times would be "heady, highminded, . . . ever learning, and never able to come to the knowledge of the truth."[24] Perhaps the educators of my generation who wrote God out of education, leaving it with no unifying principle, are more to blame for present-day student revolt than the students.

You and Your Civil Authorities

As God gave to fathers the place of authority in the home, He gave to civil powers authority in the state. Sometimes evil men abuse these two kinds of authority, but they are still the only way a society, made up of depraved human beings, can function.

The Bible is definite and explicit in its description of what the Christian's attitude should be to civil authority. It urges Christians to take the viewpoint which Christ took when the chief priest tried to trap Him into revolt against those in authority over Him. He took a coin representing tax money and, to their question about the legality of paying tribute to Caesar, he answered, after pointing to the head of Caesar on the coin, "Render therefore unto Caesar the things which be Caesar's, and unto God the things which be God's."[25] The Son of God is saying to us that unless civil authorities command us contrary to divine commands, we are to obey them. Paul urged the people of the early church to "be subject to principalities and powers; [and] to obey magistrates."[26] "Let every person be loyally subject to governing (civil) authorities."[27]

Space makes it impossible to develop the subject more fully here. Suffice it to say that in the Christian view of society, the individual has an obligation to obey and give due respect to civil authorities. The Christian citizen, unless the state interferes with his obligations toward God, should be a law-abiding, co-operative member of his society, contributing his share of money to the civil coffers, and keeping the laws of the land. In the book of Judges, "there was no king in Israel, but every man did that which was right in his own eyes."[28] The same kind of anarchy is happening today because our society too is inclined to lawlessness and disdain for civil authority.

Paul makes it clear that the Christian should be free to speak out for his rights, which is exactly what he did when he used his Roman citizenship to plead for a fair trial.[29] Peter and John, who showed that it is legitimate for a Christian to disobey civil authorities when they infringe upon religious liberties, were warned by civil authorities "not to speak at all nor teach in the name of Jesus."[30] They told the authorities that they could not obey such a command and instead prayed for courage to speak the word of God. The designation of authority is clear. Submission to proper authority, then, reveals Christian character—not weakness but strength. Henry Clay stated, "Government is a trust, and the officers of the government are trustees; and both the trust and the trustees are created for the benefit of the people."[31] This is the case of a government resting upon the principles of Christian ethics, as was true when Clay made the statement in 1829.

30

What Should My Church Relationships Mean to Me?

A MAN OF MY ACQUAINTANCE, formerly a churchgoer and now an agnostic, one day began to describe the church he had attended in his youth. "The church is a comical gathering," he chuckled, lumping all churches into the same category. "It is a collection of little power groups all trying to be the in-group. Everyone seems to be intent on tearing down the other fellow and pushing himself ahead." This is what the church meant to him. What does it mean to you and to me? Perhaps today many churches could be described as activity centers. This modern trend leads many to ask the following questions:

"HOW CAN I AVOID OVERACTIVITY IN THE CHURCH?"

Everywhere I go I hear Christians expressing concern because their church activities conflict with their home responsibilities. Whenever I speak about family responsibility, someone always asks, "How can we do the job of raising our families which you have suggested when we are so busy in the church?" My answer comes straight from experience. Soon after I became a minister's wife at the age of twenty-five, I found myself flat on my back in bed from overinvolvement in the church. I learned then how to say *no*! It is a hard lesson but one which any member of the active churches of today must learn if family life and physical health are to be preserved. "But we should serve in the church," they will say, "and I feel guilty when I say no." "I know you do," I reply, "because that was my attitude too."

Then I recount the experience which taught me about specialized service in the church. While working my way through Bible college, I was employed part time in a bookstore. During the Christmas rush my employer assigned to me the task of serving customers who needed general greeting cards. These items were packed away at the back of the store to make room for Christmas stock, and I was told to stand nearby, ready to serve anyone who needed them. My employer warned that, even if I had no customers, I must not involve myself with anything else.

As the Christmas rush increased, everyone around me was caught up in it while I stood doing my seemingly unimportant duty. At times customers tried to involve me in serving them with other purchases, but I remained faithful to my boss' instructions for some time. Finally, after a few irate comments from Christmas-card customers and other harassed clerks, I gave in to pressure. Soon I became deeply involved in the Christmas-card department and couldn't seem to escape to my assigned post.

Late that day I saw my boss coming toward me, bristling with irritation. "What are you doing here, when I asked you to stay there?" he said, emphatically pointing to where I was supposed to be. "One of my best customers just left the store, angry because she could not find shower invitations." I tried to explain the pressures that made me leave my job to do someone else's, but no excuse worked.

After I temporarily broke my health with overinvolvement in the church, I read Paul's two passages about specialized ministries in the church.[1] He writes about the different gifts and tells us to concentrate on using and improving them: "If our gift is preaching, let us preach to the limit of our vision. If it is serving others let us concentrate on our service; if it is teaching let us give all we have to our teaching; and if our gift be the stimulating of the faith of others let us set ourselves to it. Let the man who is called to give, give freely; let the man who wields authority [an administrator] think of his responsibility; and let the man who feels sympathy for his fellows act cheerfully."[2] When I read this passage, I remembered my bookshop experience. Before I recovered from my illness, I recognized my special gift and since have concentrated on it. Dr. Clyde Narramore emphasizes this truth in his book *How to Succeed in Family Living.*

"What Should I Expect from My Relationships with Members in the Church?"

Much is said in the Bible about relationships with other members in the church. Church members are urged not to be snobbish nor to give preference to wealthy members who arrive in fine apparel, while depreciating the poor who have no fine clothes.[3] Christians are also instructed not to speak evil of other members, backbiting, gossiping and criticizing them.[4] Holding grudges against fellow members is also frowned upon as hurtful to church unity.[5]

The church should be a place where individuals are befriended, encouraged, admonished and challenged, and where there is deep and honest communication. "If a brother be overtaken in a fault," Paul wrote to the church at Galatia, "ye which are spiritual, restore such an one in the spirit of meekness; considering thyself, lest thou also be tempted."[6] James said, "Confess your faults one to another, and pray one for another, that ye may be healed."[7] "Bear ye one another's burdens,"[8] we read in one Scripture verse speaking of Christian sympathy and sharing in trouble. "Every man shall bear his own burden,"[9] says another verse which refers to each accepting his own responsibilities.

There is much more, and a full study of creative relationships in a church group would be quite revealing. Modern group therapy has helped many to mental health. The church, if it were functioning as God intended, would be a warm, honest, intimate group providing both spiritual and psychological support to its members. Instead, we are often only intent on making a good impression at the expense of honest communication.

"What Should My Attitude Be Toward Church Administrators?"

As God provided fathers for the place of authority in the home, and civil leaders for the place of authority in the state, so He has called pastors, elders and deacons as leaders in the church. "Obey them that have the rule over you, and submit yourselves: for they watch for your souls, as they that must give account, that they may do it with joy, and not with grief: for that is unprofitable for you."[10]

As with husbands and wives, if pastors and people have a good relationship, authority will not have to be used often, for when there is a difference of opinion there will be communication resulting in agreement. However, even as the husband has the authority to make the final decision when there is a deadlock in the home, in the church the pastor and church leaders are in a position of authority over other church members when differences must be solved. Pastors are urged, however, not to be lifted up with pride, and church leaders are told to use their office well.[11] The church has great possibilities for helping individuals through creative spiritual relationships, but we fall far short of what God intended.

31

Should I Be an Influence on
Contemporary Society?

Too OFTEN the Christians in today's society are written off as
an inconsequential minority who are not quite "with it." I believe, if we study the influence exerted by the early Christians
we will readily admit that our secular society's evaluation of us
is our own fault.

Pitirim Sorokin is called "the world's greatest sociologist"
by one of his biographers. In his book *The Crisis of Our Age*
Sorokin compares the Roman world, into which the young
church was born, with our society.[1] The similarity of the two
cultures is astounding. The callousness of Rome compares well
with our modern alienation and violence, and Rome's sensuality
is almost identical with our society's emphasis on the appetites
of the body. The lust for power in Rome resembles our driving
passion for success, recognition and material gain. Karen
Horney in her book *The Neurotic Personality of Our Time* describes the dynamics behind our two driving passions, our com-
pulsion to be loved, often neurotically expressed in extreme
sexuality, and our quest for power, neurotically expressed in a
passionate competitiveness.[2] These are the symptoms of our
deep anxiety.

Into such a culture the young church was born on the day of
Pentecost. Just twenty years later, the people in Thessalonica,
six hundred miles of primitive travel away, said in desperation,
"These that have turned the world upside down are come hither
also."[3] How had so few made such an impact on their society
in so short a time? Unlike modern Christianity, they were not a

subculture. Instead they were vital participants in every area of contemporary life, infiltrating all of their society with their vibrant lives and message. Here is the result after thirty years of their history.

THE EARLY CHRISTIAN IMPACT ON RELIGIOUS LIFE

Although we sometimes consider religion and Christianity synonymously, they can be diametrically opposed. The early Christians made an impact on the religious life of their times. The spiritualists of their day were upset because a girl whom they used as a sorcerer or medium was healed and was no longer available for sorceries.[4]

Paul, a Ph.D. of his day and the leader of the religious opposition against Christianity, believed on the risen Christ and joined the little band of Christians as their most militant leader.[5] Crispus, the chief ruler of the synagogue at Corinth, believed and was baptized with his family.[6] Many Hebrew priests at Jerusalem believed the Christian message.[7]

THE EARLY CHRISTIAN IMPACT ON EDUCATIONAL LIFE

Members of the young church made an impact on contemporary thought. Paul, a graduate of the university where Gamaliel was the teacher, became a leader in early apologetics. Gamaliel is believed to have been president of the Sanhedrin (the Jewish governing body) and was an outstanding scholar.[8] Because of Paul's contacts with such scholars, he took his place in discussions with the intellectuals, arguing the claims of Christianity with all who came to learn. Some believed and joined Paul. At Mars Hill in Athens he reasoned with the intellectuals, quoting from their own poets, and some believed.[9] Dr. John Haggai in chapter 18 of his book *How to Win over Worry* enlarges on the impact and relevance of Paul's lecture. At Ephesus he went into the synagogue for three months and brought the Christian message to the doctors there, persuading them of the things of the kingdom of God,[10] and then he moved to one of the famous schools of his day of which Tyrannus was the teacher.[11] There he presented the Christian message to contemporary thinkers and involved them in dialogue.

THE EARLY CHRISTIAN IMPACT ON GOVERNMENTAL LIFE

Governmental life did not escape the influence of the young church. The sermon given by Stephen, the first martyr of the church, is a dynamic presentation of the cause of God. The leaders present were not able to resist the wisdom of the spirit by which he spoke. In fact, that sermon was so effective that it cost him his life.[12] The treasurer of Ethiopia, who had perhaps heard the message of Christ in his own language at Pentecost, visited Jerusalem another year for the feast. On his way home, he was reached by Philip, accepted the risen Christ as his Saviour, and was baptized before all his retinue of servants and attendants.[13] Agrippa, ruler of Judea, accompanied by the chief captains of his army and the principal men of the city of Caesarea, heard Paul's account of his conversion. Agrippa was moved to cry, "Almost thou persuadest me to be a Christian." Beside him in the court sat his sister Bernice, with whom he lived in an incestuous relationship. This perhaps explains why he was almost and not altogether persuaded.[14] Felix, procurator of Judea, and his wife, Drusilla, heard Paul's message as he gave his defense before them. Alarmed and terrified, Felix cried out, "Go thy way for this time; when I have a convenient season I will call thee." Festus, successor to Felix, heard Paul and cried, "Paul, thou art beside thyself; much learning doth make thee mad."[15] Publius, the chief man of the island of Melita, honored Paul because his father had been healed after Paul prayed for him.[16] Julius, the Roman centurion who was in charge of Paul as they traveled by ship to Rome, was impressed with the power of God in the life of Paul because of his faith and peace in the face of shipwreck and danger.[17]

Working in the household of Caesar were Christians, perhaps slaves, who had been liberated spiritually and were members of the infant church.[18] At Philippi the governor of the jail believed on Jesus Christ, and he and his family were baptized.[19] Cornelius the centurion became a Christian and invited a large group of his relatives and friends to his house so the apostle Peter could teach them more about their new faith.[20] So government leaders of the early Christian era became well acquainted with the message of the virile young church.

THE EARLY CHRISTIAN IMPACT ON BUSINESS LIFE

Early Christians also had an effect on the business life of their society. Lydia, the first European convert and a wealthy Jewish proselyte, accepted Jesus Christ as her Saviour and opened her home to the apostle Paul.[21] At Joppa, Peter stayed with Simon the tanner, whose house was by the seaside, and apparently Simon became a member of the early church.[22] Aquila and Priscilla, who owned a tent-making business in Corinth, housed Paul while he began the church at Corinth. They were devoted disciples.[23] The Christians upset one flourishing business at Ephesus because too many people were leaving the worship of Diana to follow Christ. The silversmiths "made silver shrines for Diana, [which] brought no small gain unto the craftsmen." Concerned because they feared that their craft was "in danger to be set at nought," they called a convention of all silversmiths to try to solve the problem which the power of Christianity had created for their industry.[24]

THE EARLY CHRISTIAN IMPACT ON THE CRIMINAL SEGMENT

The criminal segment of society was also affected by the spread of Christianity. In the church at Corinth, as in other churches, were former criminals now living a law-abiding life. The city contained thieves and extortioners, not to mention the immoral, drunkards, and practicing homosexuals, of whom Paul said, "Such were some of you: but [now] ye are washed."[25] Onesimus, a young slave who had run away with his master's goods, met Paul at Rome and although he had been "unprofitable," he found God and became profitable to both Paul and his master.[26]

Why Is Christian Impact on Our Society So Limited?

This is only a part of what was accomplished as the early Christians infiltrated their society with the message of salvation. Why were they so effective and we so ineffective? They had no mass communications, no rapid transit, no air travel, no printing press. They had no modern facilities and no trained ministry. Instead they had a community violently hostile to their cause and no previous generation from which to gain a following. Yet a nucleus of 120 reached their world in about thirty years. Why are we so ineffective?

OUR ATTITUDES ARE DIFFERENT

Our attitude to people is different. The early Christians "cared" and it was this compassion that drew people to their ranks. In the callous Roman society, love was attractive. It could be just as attractive in our society of the "lonely crowd."[27] Today, especially in our great urban centers, people feel alienated and lonely. In an earlier day, almost every individual had people to whom he mattered. The family doctor, the corner grocer, relatives, neighbors and friends all showed concern for the individual. Now the doctor has become a cog in the great wheel of medical practice, a specialist who never saw you before and perhaps never will again. There is no relationship with a kind family doctor for most lonely people. Those in need often fail to receive the help of neighbors or friends, only the business-like contact of a social worker carrying a food voucher or a requisition for rent money. Friends and neighbors and even relatives are too busy succeeding to communicate in depth. In all of this is our opportunity to win people with compassionate Christianity. But we exhibit no more compassion than the non-Christian because we are too busy organizing our church programs.

OUR CHARACTER IS DIFFERENT

Our character is different too. We are not as interested in integrity, honesty, humility, and Christ-centeredness as they were.

We also know very little about contentment. The early Christians "did eat their meat with gladness and singleness of heart, praising God, and having favour with all the people. And the Lord added to the church daily such as should be saved."[28] Their character differed from ours and attracted others.

OUR CONCEPTS ARE DIFFERENT

Our concept of Christianity is also different from theirs. They saw their task as reaching their world through individual contacts, but we see it as a group effort. They believed in contact and made sympathetic approaches to people; we emphasize differences and are known for what we *don't* do. They believed in being separated from the attitudes and practices of their godless society; we believe in being isolated from the people in our world.

Joseph Bayly pictures us realistically in his book *The Gospel Blimp.*[29] We try to people our little world with Christians— we choose a Christian doctor, a Christian lawyer, a Christian real estate broker and, if we could, would fill the houses on our street with Christian families. We have our recreation with church people, do our business with church people, choose all our associates from church people, and then wonder why we are not reaching the unchurched. We do this under the guise of separation from the world. It is not separation, but isolation. Christ sat down with sinners but was separate from them.[30] The early Christians were not isolated but they were much less influenced by the behavior and attitudes of their world. We sometimes choose isolation to protect ourselves from attack or embarrassment.

The early Christians saw Christianity as a vital relationship with God. We sometimes view it as the keeping of rules and forms and time-worn traditions. They were "be-ers," we are "do-ers." They loved and won the hearts of outsiders. Stephen, with his face shining, prayed for his enemies as he died. Paul never forgot that.[31] Paul and Silas sang praises to God in the Philippian jail rather than complaining. The jailor never forgot that.[32] The early Christians loved people and reached their hearts; we organize to fill seats and end up with full churches and empty hearts. We are certainly not turning our world upside down.

God help us to reconsider our relationship to our society in the light of the book of Acts. May our Christianity cease to be a pale reflection of that dynamic love which "turned the world upside down."

Part VIII

YOU AND YOUR GOD

32

Does God Love *Me?*

PITIRIM SOROKIN, an American sociologist who has studied and written widely on the subject of love, describes it thus in his book, *The Ways and Power of Love:*

> Love is the experience that annuls our individual loneliness, fills the emptiness of our isolation with the richest value, breaks and transcends the narrow walls of our little egos and makes us co-participants in the highest life of humanity thus expanding our true individuality. It is a life giving force—the more one's love expands the greater are the returns that replenish its expenditure. Studies show that altruists live longer than egoists and that empty loneliness is the main cause of suicide. Love makes fearless and powerful feelings. The more selfish I make myself the greater will be my fear.[1]

The Bible made a similar statement long ago, "Perfect love casteth out fear."[2] Where can we find perfect love?

PERFECT LOVE

Sorokin gives us a clue when he says, "There are people with unexplained powers of love for which they seem to have no source of love energy. Their love can only be explained by an intangible, little-studied source called God, the Heavenly Father. When a person knows how to release these forces of love energy he can spend lavishly without exhausting his supply. Love is reinforced miraculously by prayer."[3]

Sorokin gives what he considers the five dimensions of love.[4] I should like to explain Sorokin's dimensions of love and apply them to the love of God—the love that excels all human love.

The Intensity of His Love

Sorokin describes one dimension of love as *intensity* which, scaled from 0 to 100, would place indifference at zero and infinite intensity at 100. Intensity of love is seen in actions. In a relationship which has love feelings close to indifference the actions involve the giving of lesser values. For example, a person may give his seat on a streetcar to an elderly person because he has a small measure of care for that person. When love is intense, it is measured by the giving of our greatest values—time, ambitions, strength, possessions and, in rare cases, even life. Rosa Thorpe's beautiful poem "Curfew Must Not Ring Tonight" illustrates intense love—a young man is condemned to death at the ringing of curfew, and his sweetheart clings to the clapper of the huge bell so that the curfew does not ring. Since the sexton is deaf, he is unaware of the bell's silence. The prisoner's life is saved by his friend's sacrifice. Her bruised body depicts the intensity of her love.

In this dimension God's love excels all others. God the Father was willing to give His cherished Son to die for us. God the Son was willing to give up His relationship with His Father, His reputation, His friends, His family, His physical comfort, and finally His life.

The Extensity of His Love

Sorokin also measures love with the yardstick of extensity. In this dimension of love, people vary a great deal. Some only extend their love to one other individual, others to their immediate family, while still others are able to encompass many in their circle of love. Great altruists, such as Albert Schweitzer, extend their love to great numbers of people, but such altruistic individuals make up only a small proportion of the world's total population.

Judged by Sorokin's scale, God's love which reaches infinity in *intensity* also is infinite in *extensity*. The Bible not only describes God as a Person who loves intensely (God so loved . . .

that He gave His only begotten Son) but also as a Person who loves to the infinite limit of *extensity.* "God so loved *the world*"[5] —the scope of His caring includes all people of all time.

THE DURATION OF HIS LOVE

The duration of love may range from the shortest moment to a whole lifetime, Sorokin observes. It is affected by several factors. Separation from a love object can shorten the duration of love even though at the time it seemed to be an intense feeling. Many teenagers, away on a summer vacation, have met a friend and experienced deep feelings of love for this person. After returning home, the intense feelings of the vacation period waned to complete indifference. They did not endure the strain of separation.

Another factor that affects the duration of love is reciprocation on the part of the loved person. Love's energy is replenished by a return of love, so unrequited human love usually does not last long. A young man may fall in love with a girl, but if he receives no response from her, the duration of his love will be limited.

Divine love, if we accept the biblical concept of God, is everlasting. Time, space, and lack of response from the love object do not affect God's ability to love. In Jeremiah, God tells His people who had been most rebellious and rejecting of Him, "I have loved thee with an everlasting love; therefore with lovingkindness have I drawn thee."[6] John reports of Jesus Christ that "having loved his own . . . he loved them unto the end."[7]

THE PURITY OF HIS LOVE

Sorokin describes this dimension as ranging from the sullied kind of love for which the motive is utility, pleasure, advantage or profit, to the unselfish, giving love which knows no bargain or reward. Some human love is only the thinnest trickle in a muddy current of selfish aspirations and purposes. This kind of love is fragile and lacks both intensity and duration. It is well illustrated by the people who love only because they have common enemies.

God's love is absolutely pure; since He is complete and autonomous in His personality, He does not love out of any need to gain advantage or to use the love object to further His ends. His love is not, like so much of human love, an extension of self-love. Therefore, His love never exploits its object.

God also has infinite wisdom. His love is aware of our needs, our future, our weaknesses and our strengths. He is never like some human beings, well intentioned but damaging in their expressions of love. Trusting ourselves to Him is both safe and profitable, for an intimate relationship with God frees us for fulfillment. Goethe said, "The greatest good is to find a person of superior qualities and love him supremely." God is that Person.

The Adequacy of His Love

Adequacy when applied to love has to do with its effects on the love object. Some love, while subjectively genuine in the loving person, has objective consequences which are different or even opposite to the love goal. For example, a loving mother may wish to make her child a lovable, honest, industrious person. If her love is inadequate, she will pamper him, satisfying all his desires and neglecting to discipline him. In the end, the object of her love becomes a self-centered, irresponsible, lazy, dishonest individual. The objective consequences of her love are thus opposite to its goals.

God's love is adequate. The Scriptures picture Him as one who "corrects and disciplines every one whom He loves, and He punishes . . . every son whom He accepts and welcomes to His heart and cherishes."[8]

In other passages God is shown to be the kind of Father who does not shield his children from maturing experiences but allows "fiery trials."[9]

Because God's love is adequate, it has never failed to transform the person given over to its power.

THE PERSONALITY THAT HAS DEEP ROOTS AND FIRM FOUNDATIONS IN GOD'S LOVE

God's love is the ultimate in every dimension—infinite in intensity, all-encompassing in extensity, eternal in duration, self-emptying in purity, and all-transforming in adequacy. No wonder Paul prayed that we might be able to comprehend "what is the breadth, and length, and depth, and height; and to know the love of Christ, which passeth knowledge, that we might be filled with all the fullness of God."[10] This love can become the deep roots and firm foundations of one's personality, he notes in the same passage.[11] His love will enhance and position every other relationship. To the person whose social direction is toward people, it will be a protection against inordinate or greedy affections; to the person who moves against people, it becomes an antidote for hatred and hostility; and to the person who moves away from people, it is an escape from loveless indifference.

In God alone is perfect love, and a relationship with Him supersedes all others.

33

What Is an Intimate Relationship with God Like?

THIS PERFECT five-dimensional love of God is coldly abstract until it is placed in the context of a relationship. We are all like the little girl who kept calling out anxiously for her mother when she was supposed to be asleep. Finally the exasperated mother, hoping to comfort her, said, "You don't have to be afraid, dear. Didn't you ask God to 'keep you till the morning light'? He will take care of you."

"But Mommy," the child wailed, "I want somebody with a face." The biblical description of God's relationship with human beings gives Him a face.

HE HAS THE FACE OF A FATHER

Most adults have some memory of the comfort of a father's strong arms. "Like as a father pitieth his children," the Bible says, "so the LORD pitieth them that fear him."[1] But God does not allow His feelings of pity to lower His expectations. Otherwise He would not be a true Father. He wants us to grow in maturity that we may enjoy its fruits.

The experience of Jacob illustrates God's father love. Jacob's human fathering was annulled by his protective and manipulating mother who doted on him. Deceiving her own husband, she got Jacob the place of advantage when she helped him steal his brother's heritage. Then God used Esau, who was still angered by Jacob's exploitation, to cut Jacob loose from his mother's apron strings.

Jacob learned the hard way that his mother was not God, even though she tried to be. God pitied this pampered youth as he settled down for his first night away from home. Jacob faced reality for the first time in his life—the stone pillow, the lonely night, the restless sounds of prowling beasts, and the awesome realization of God's presence. God's father love used these as reality therapy. The same love engineered a meeting with his conniving Uncle Laban. In Laban, God "set him up a glass where he might see the innermost part of himself."[2] Here, for fourteen years, he grew in self-awareness. All the while, God's father love sustained him.

Years later, he humbly returned home to his mother's empty chair and his brother's kind forgiveness—no longer Jacob the supplanter, but Israel a prince with God.

HE HAS THE FACE OF A MOTHER

Although God is never referred to as a mother, one of the the names of God in the Old Testament is El Shaddai—the breasted God who nourishes, gives strength and satisfies.[3] Elijah exemplifies this role of God. After the prophet fled from a pursuing Jezebel, he sat under a juniper tree in the wilderness and told God that life was just too much. He was in a state of total exhaustion.

God did not treat him as a failure but gave him a supper of quail meat and put him to sleep. When he awoke, Elijah was a new man—refreshed physically and emotionally. Life no longer seemed too much for he had experienced the understanding and comfort of God's nurturing.

HE HAS THE FACE OF A FRIEND

Three times in Scripture Abraham is called the friend of God. The quality peculiar to the love of a friend is faithful counsel. "Ointment and perfume rejoice the heart," the wise man observed, "so doth the sweetness of a man's friend by hearty counsel."[4] If any man needed guidance and counsel, it was Abraham. Having left the Chaldean city of Ur to embark on a journey with an unknown destination, he learned to appreciate God as a Friend who was always there to give counsel.

He Has the Face of a Lover or Husband

A person can love many friends but only one lover simultaneously. The nature of this relationship eliminates other lovers. When the Bible speaks of God as a jealous God, it refers to our relationship to Him as a lover who is satisfied only with first place in our affections. Hosea's experience illustrates this aspect of the love of God. With patience and compassion he woos his wayward wife, Gomer, away from her false lovers. Along with this personal struggle of Hosea runs a secondary plot, the story of Israel's wanderings from their loving God. "Rejoice not, O Israel, for joy, as other people: for thou hast gone a whoring from thy God," the prophet called out.[5] At the end of the book, both Gomer and Israel return—Gomer to Hosea and Israel to their God.

He Has the Face of a Brother

A ragged Korean orphan was seen one day struggling along a rubble-scattered street with his little brother on his back. A bystander, observing the emaciated child staggering along, said to him, "You have quite a burden to carry." "He's not a burden," the boy replied, "he's my brother."

Joseph presents this same picture. Though cruelly and unjustly treated, he returns good for evil and loyalty for disloyalty. Weeping with compassion, he saves his brothers from starvation and himself from isolation. Jesus Christ is described as our elder brother.

The All-Inclusive Relationship

If we could add the qualities of every kind of human relationship, and multiply the total by the infinite perfection of deity, then subtract all the sorrows flowing from human selfishness, and multiply the result by eternity, we might have a small fraction of the quality of the relationship which God offers to any human being who will come to Him.

Even if life has been filled with broken relationships and social and spiritual failure, His perfect love can "bind up the broken-hearted."[6] He can "give unto them beauty for ashes, the oil of joy for mourning, the garment of praise for the spirit of heaviness."[7]

Perhaps our human relationships are happy and fulfilling; yet, without a relationship with God, we are social paupers.

Father! Mother! Wife! Husband! Son! Daughter! Lover! Friend! They are the source of our most exquisite joys and our most excruciating sorrows—the pulse of life—the ebb and flow of existence. In relationships we give ourselves away, only to find ourselves again, twofold more the child of hell—or heaven. Into our relationships we empty the bitter pools of our gnarled resentments, the cluttered springs of our selfish caring, the slimy wells of our human degradation. All poured pell-mell upon our fellows along with our love—the bitter with the sweet. Now destroying, now creating, we vent ourselves arbitrarily like ambivalent demigods.

Then from a cross comes that pure stream of God's love. A door opens reluctantly within us. He indwells our innermost caverns, flowing out of us to others in loving relationships. Enemies and friends, lovely and unlovely, deserving and undeserving, black and white, all feel the impact of our cleansed caring.

John says, "If we love one another, God dwelleth in us, and his love is perfected in us."[8] This is not a secondary theme of Christianity; it is its essence. Vital Christianity is born in relationship with God and expressed in relationships with others. That is why You and Yours is such an urgent matter.

Notes

CHAPTER 1

1. Clifford Morgan, *Introduction to Psychology*, p. 66.
2. 1 Pe 5:6.
3. Ro 12:3, Amplified.
4. Mt 19:19, Amplified.
5. 2 Ti 4:7-8.
6. Gen 2:18.

CHAPTER 2

1. 1 Ti 2:14.
2. S. Freud, *An Outline of Psychoanalysis*, chaps 1, 2, 8; Calvin Hall, *A Primer of Freudian Psychology*, pp. 22-27.
3. Jer 17:9.
4. Ps 44:21.
5. 1 Sa 2:3.
6. Walter J. Coville et al. *Abnormal Psychology*, p. 29.
7. Ro 5:12.
8. Mk 7:15.
9. Ja 1:13-15.
10. W. F. Ogburn and M. F. Nimkoff, *Sociology*, p. 258; Coville et al., pp. 33-34.
11. Heb 12:1, Amplified.
12. Mk 15:10.
13. Lk 18:11.
14. 3 Jn 9.
15. *MacBeth*, act 5, scene 1.
16. Ro 7:15, 24-25, Amplified.

CHAPTER 3

1. Ro 7:21, Amplified.
2. Ro 2:14-15.
3. W. F. Ogburn and M. F. Nimkoff, *Sociology*, pp. 309-10.
4. Ro 2:14-15.
5. Walter J. Coville et al., *Abnormal Psychology*, pp. 126-27.
6. Col 3:21, Amplified.
7. Pr 29:17.
8. Ro 7:25, Amplified.
9. Heb 4:15.
10. Mt 4:7, Amplified.
11. Mt 27:42-43.
12. Ro 8:1.
13. Jn 3:17-18.
14. Ro 7:24-25, Amplified.
15. Phil 1:21, NEB.

CHAPTER 4

1. Jn 21:15.
2. Ro 12:2.
3. Ro 12:2, Phillips.

CHAPTER 5

1. 1 Co 7:9.
2. 1 Co 7:8, Amplified.
3. 1 Th 4:3-5, American Trans.
4. Paul H. Landis, *Making the Most of Marriage*, p. 535.

CHAPTER 6

1. Ps 127:3.
2. Erich Fromm, *The Art of Loving*, p. 22.
3. 1 Ti 5:8.
4. Eph 4:26.

CHAPTER 7

1. 1 Th 5:23, Amplified.
2. Paul H. Landis, *Making the Most of Marriage*, p. 282.
3. Lewis Terman, *Psychological Factors in Marital Happiness*.
4. Amos 3:3.
5. 1 Th 4:3-6, Amplified.
6. Phillip Polatine and Ellen Philtine, *Marriage in the Modern World*, p. 52.
7. Lester A. Kirkendall, "Premarital Sex Relations, The Problem and Its Implications," *Pastoral Psychology* (Apr. 1956).
8. E. E. LeMasters, *Modern Courtship and Marriage*, pp. 195-96.
9. William R. Reevey, "Premarital Petting Behaviour and Marital Happiness Predictions," *Marriage and Family Living* (Nov. 1959).
10. Landis, p. 396.
11. Alfred C. Kinsey, *Sexual Behavior in the Human Female,* pp. 427-31.
12. Christine Hillman, "An Advice Column's Challenge for Family Life Education," *Marriage and Family Living* (Feb. 1954).
13. Landis, chap. 20; and Evelyn M. Duvall, *Why Wait Till Marriage?* and *Love and the Facts of Life*; Charlie Shedd, *The Stork Is Dead.*
14. Eph 5:31; Gen. 2:24.
15. Erich Fromm, *The Art of Loving*, pp. 23-24.
16. Eph 5:33, Amplified.

CHAPTER 8

1. Pr 18:22.

CHAPTER 9

1. Deu 24:5.
2. Paul H. Landis, *Making the Most of Marriage*, pp. 419-20.
3. Mt 19:4; Mk 10:6.

CHAPTER 10

1. See these books on the subject: Van De Velde, *The Ideal Marriage*; and Herbert J. Miles, *Sexual Happiness in Marriage*.
2. 1 Co 7:3-5, Amplified.

CHAPTER 11

1. Eph 4:2, Phillips.
2. Col 3:19, Amplified.

CHAPTER 12

1. Phil 4:11.
2. Pr 27:15.
3. Pr 21:19.
4. Eph 5:33, Amplified.
5. Eph 5:22, Amplified.

CHAPTER 13

1. Gen 2:24; Mt 19:5; Mk 10:7.
2. Paul H. Landis, "Length of Time Required to Achieve Adjustment in Marriage," *American Sociological Review* (Dec. 1946).
3. Evelyn M. Duvall, *In-Laws: Pro and Con*, pp. 4, 197.

CHAPTER 16

1. Phillip Polatine and Ellen Philtine, *Marriage in the Modern World*, p. 224.
2. Louis H. Burke, *With This Ring*.

CHAPTER 17

1. Edmund Bergler, *The Revolt of the Middle Aged Man*, Preface.
2. Marion Hilliard, *A Woman Doctor Looks at Love and Life*, p. 148.

CHAPTER 18

1. John Bowlby, *Child Care and the Growth of Love*, p. 36.
2. Eph 6:4, Amplified.

CHAPTER 19

1. Irene M. Josselyn, *The Psychosocial Development of Children*, pp. 91-92.

CHAPTER 20

1. Pr 22:6.
2. Pr 22:6, Amplified.
3. Lk 2:52.
4. 1 Co 9:25-27.
5. Lk 2:41-47.
6. 2 Ti 3:4, KJV and Amplified.
7. Edwin H. Rian, *Christianity and American Education*, chap. 11.
8. Jn 1:13.
9. Jn 3:17.
10. Heb 1:3.
11. Ps 19:3.

CHAPTER 21

1. Ro 12:10, Amplified.
2. Phil 2:4, Amplified.
3. Eph 4:28, Amplified.
4. Lk 13:34.
5. Frances L. Ilg and Louise Bates Ames, *The Gesell Institute's Child Behaviour*.
6. Lam 3:27.
7. These concepts were first presented by Karen Horney.

8. 2 Co 9:6.
9. Ec 11:1.
10. Mt 6:19-21.
11. Eph 6:5-6.

CHAPTER 23

1. Is 30:15.
2. Gen 2:24; Mt 19:5; Eph 5:31.
3. Ex 20:12.
4. 1 Ti 3:3, Amplified.
5. 1 Ti 6:9-10, Amplified.

CHAPTER 24

1. Pr 3:5-6.
2. Heb 11:24-25.
3. Phil 3:14-15, Amplified.

CHAPTER 25

1. 1 Th 1:2-3.

CHAPTER 26

1. Eph 6:1; Col 3:20.
2. Pr 10:1.
3. Lk 2:51.
4. Erich Fromm, *The Art of Loving*, pp. 35-36.
5. Eph 6:4.
6. Pr 13:1.
7. Pr 22:6.

CHAPTER 27

1. Pr 17:17.
2. Heb 12:15.
3. 2 Ti 1:5, Amplified.

CHAPTER 28

1. 1 Sa 18:1.
2. Pr 17:17.
3. Pr 27:6.
4. Pr 27:17.
5. Erich Fromm, *The Art of Loving*, pp. 15-17.

CHAPTER 29

1. Titus 3:8, Amplified.
2. Eph 6:5-7, Amplified.
3. Titus 2:10, Amplified.
4. 1 Pe 2:18, Amplified.
5. Eph 6:9-10, Amplified.
6. Lev 19:13.
7. Lev 25:43.
8. Deu 24:14.
9. Col 4:1.
10. 1 Ti 5:18.
11. Ja 5:4.
12. Ja 5:9, Amplified.

13. Lam 5:8.
14. Michael Demiashkevitch, *An Introduction to the Philosophy of Education*, pp. 339-42.
15. 1 Pe 5:5.
16. Pr 23:12.
17. B. B. Bogoslavsky, *The Ideal School*, p. 131.
18. Ja 1:19.
19. Job 12:12.
20. Ps 111:10; Pr 1:7; 9:10.
21. Edwin H. Rian, *Christianity and American Education*, chap. 11.
22. Harvard Committee, *General Education in a Free Society*, p. 39.
23. Walter Lippman, "Education Versus Western Civilization," *American Scholar* (Spring, 1941).
24. 2 Ti 3:4, 7.
25. Lk 20:25.
26. Titus 3:1.
27. Ro 13:1*a*, Amplified.
28. Judg 17:6.
29. Ac 22:25.
30. Ac 4:18-29.
31. Lewis C. Henry, *Five Thousand Quotations*, p. 111.

CHAPTER 30

1. Ro 12:6-8; 1 Co 12:4-11.
2. Ro 12:6-8, Phillips.
3. Ja 2:2-3.
4. Ja 4:11.
5. Ja 5:9.
6. Gal 6:1.
7. Ja 5:16.
8. Gal 6:2.
9. Gal 6:5.
10. Heb 13:17.
11. 1 Ti 3:13.

CHAPTER 31

1. Pitirim Sorokin, *The Crisis of Our Age.*
2. Karen Horney, *The Neurotic Personality of Our Time.*
3. Ac 17:6.
4. Ac 16:16-24.
5. Ac 9.
6. Ac 18:8; 1 Co 1:14.
7. Ac 6:7.
8. Ac 22:3; 5:34.
9. Ac 17:15-34.
10. Ac 19:8-9.
11. Ac 19:8-10.
12. Ac 6:10; 7:54.
13. Ac 8:26-39.
14. Ac 26.
15. Ac 26:25-26; 24:24-27.
16. Ac 28:7-10.
17. Ac 27.
18. Phil 4:22.
19. Ac 16:25-40.

20. Ac 10:17-48.
21. Ac 16:14, 40.
22. Ac 9:43; 10:6.
23. Ac 18:2, 18-19.
24. Ac 19:23-41.
25. 1 Co 6:9-11.
26. Phile 1:11.
27. David Riesman, *The Lonely Crowd.*
28. Ac 2:46-47.
29. Joseph T. Bayly, *The Gospel Blimp.*
30. Cf. Mt 9:10; Heb 7:26.
31. Ac 7.
32. Ac 16:25-34.

CHAPTER 32

1. Pitirim Sorokin, *The Ways and Power of Love*, chap. 1.
2. 1 Jn 4:18.
3. Sorokin, chap. 2.
4. Ibid.
5. Jn 3:16.
6. Jer 31:3.
7. Jn 13:1.
8. Heb 12:6, Amplified.
9. 1 Pe 4:12.
10. Eph 3:18-19.
11. Eph 3:17, Amplified.

CHAPTER 33

1. Ps 103:13.
2. *Hamlet*, act 3, scene 4.
3. Gen 17:1; Isa 66:13.
4. Pr 27:9.
5. Ho 9:1.
6. Is 61:1.
7. Is 61:3.
8. 1 Jn 4:12.

Bibliography

Adcok, C. J. *Fundamentals of Psychology.* Baltimore: Pelican Books, 1964.

Adler, Alfred. *Understanding Human Nature.* London: Allen & Unwin, 1928 (New York: Fawcett, 1963).

Allen, Charles L. *God's Psychiatry.* Westwood, N.J.: Revell, 1953.

Ashton, M. L. *Mind at Ease.* Fort Washington, Pa.: Christian Literature Crusade, 1961.

Babbage, Stuart Barton. *Christianity and Sex.* Chicago: Inter-Varsity, 1963.

————. *Sex and Sanity.* Philadelphia: Westminster, 1965.

Barrett, Ethel. *Sometimes I Feel Like a Blob.* Glendale, Calif.: Regal Books, 1965.

Bayly, Joe. *The Gospel Blimp.* Grand Rapids: Zondervan, 1960.

Bergler, Edmund. *The Revolt of the Middle Aged Man.* New York: Grosset & Dunlap, 1957.

Berne, Eric. *Games People Play.* New York: Grove, 1964.

Black, Hugh. *Friendship.* New York: Revell, 1898.

Blatz, William E. *Understanding the Young Child.* New York: Erwin, 1948.

Bogoslavsky, B. B. *The Ideal School.* New York: Macmillan, 1936.

Bowlby, John. *Child Care and the Growth of Love.* Baltimore: Pelican Books, 1965.

Brandt, Henry. *Christians Have Troubles Too.* Old Tappan, N.J.: Revell, 1968.

Brown, J. A. C. *Freud and the Post Freudians.* Baltimore: Pelican Books, 1961.

Bryant, Lee. *Come Fill the Cup.* Waco, Tex.: Word, 1970.

Burke, Louis H. *With This Ring.* New York: McGraw-Hill, 1958.

Byrd, Eliver Erasmus. *Family Life Source Book.* Palo Alto, Calif.: Stanford U., 1956.

Callwood, June. *Love, Hate, Fear, Anger, and other Lively Emotions.* New York: Doubleday, 1964.

Caprio, Frank S. *Female Homosexuality.* New York: Grove, Black Cat Books, 1954.

214

Cole, William G. *Sex and Love in the Bible.* New York: Association, 1959.

Coville, Walter J., et al. *Abnormal Psychology.* New York: Barnes and Noble College Outline Series, 1960.

De Beauvoir, Simone. *The Second Sex.* Toronto, Bantam Books, 1961.

Demiashkevitch, Michael. *An Introduction to the Philosophy of Education.* New York: American Book, 1935.

Drummond, Henry. *The Greatest Thing in the World.* London: Hodder and Stoughton, 1917.

Duvall, Evelyn Millis. *The Art of Dating.* New York: Association, 1958.

———. *Being Married.* New York: Association, 1962.

———. *In-laws, Pro and Con.* New York: Association, 1954.

———. *Love and the Facts of Life.* New York: Association, 1963.

———. *Sense and Nonsense About Sex.* New York: Association, 1962.

———. *Today's Teenagers.* New York: Association, 1966.

———. *Why Wait Till Marriage?* New York: Association, 1965.

Eaton, Joseph W. and Weil, Robert. *Culture and Mental Disorders.* Glencoe, Ill.: Free, 1955.

Edwards, R. H. *A Person-Minded Ministry.* Nashville, Tenn.: Cokesbury, 1940.

Eisenstein, Victor W. *Neurotic Interactions in Marriage.* London: Tavistock, 1965.

Erb, Alta Mae. *Christian Education in the Home.* Scottdale, Pa.: Herald, 1963.

Fisher, James and Hawley, Lowell. *A Few Buttons Missing.* Philadelphia: Lippincott, 1951.

Frame, John D. *Psychology and Personality Development.* Chicago: Moody, 1961.

Fromm, Erich. *The Art of Loving.* New York: Harper, 1956.

———. *Escape from Freedom.* New York: Holt, Rinehart & Winston, 1941.

———. *The Revolution of Hope.* New York: Harper, 1968.

Freud, Anna. *Psychoanalysis for Teachers and Parents.* Boston: Beacon, 1960.

Freud, Sigmund. *The Ego and the Id.* London: Hogarth, 1962.

———. *An Outline of Psychoanalysis.* London: Hogarth, 1949.

Friedan, Betty. *The Feminine Mystique.* New York: Norton, 1963.

Fyvell, T. R. *The Insecure Offenders—Rebellious Youth in the Welfare State.* Baltimore: Pelican Books, 1963.

Gessell, Arnold. *The Child from 5-10.* New York: Harper, 1946.

———. *The Years from 10-16.* New York: Harper, 1956.

Ginott, Haim. *Between Parent and Child.* New York: Macmillan, 1965.
———. *Between Parent and Teenager.* New York: Macmillan, 1969.
Gluek, Sheldon and Gluek, Eleanor. *Predicting Delinquency and Crime.* Cambridge: Harvard U., 1959.
Green, S. L. and Rothenberg, A. B. *A Manual of First Aid for Mental Health in Childhood and Adolescence.* New York: Julian, 1954.
Haggai, John Edmund. *How to Win over Worry.* Grand Rapids: Zondervan, 1959.
Hall, Calvin. *A Primer of Freudian Psychology.* New York: World, 1954.
Hart, Hornell. *The Science of Social Relations.* New York: Henry & Holt, 1927.
Harvard Committee. *On the Objectives of a General Education in a Free Society.* Cambridge: Harvard U., 1945.
Henry, Lewis C. *Five Thousand Quotations.* New York: Doubleday, 1945.
Hilliard, Marion. *A Woman Doctor Looks at Love and Life.* Toronto: Doubleday Canada, 1957.
Hillman, Christine. "An Advice Column's Challenge for Family Life Education," *Marriage and Family Living.* (Feb. 1954).
Hollinshead, A. B. *Elmtown's Youth, Science Edition.* New York: Wiley, 1949.
Hollis, Florence. *Women in Marital Conflict.* New York: Family Service Assn., 1949.
Horney, Karen. *Feminine Psychology.* New York: Norton, 1967.
———. *The Neurotic Personality of Our Time.* New York: Norton, 1937.
———. *New Ways in Psychoanalysis.* New York: Norton, 1939.
———. *Our Inner Conflict.* New York: Norton, 1945.
———. *Self-Analysis.* New York: Norton, 1946.
Ilg, Frances L. and Ames, Louise Bates, *Gesell Institute's Child Behavior.* New York: Dell, 1960.
Johnson, Wendell. *People in Quandaries.* New York: Harper, 1946.
Josselyn, Irene M. *The Adolescent and His World.* New York: Family Service Assn. of America, 1952.
———. *The Happy Child.* New York: Random House, 1955.
———. *Psychosocial Development of Children.* New York: Family Service Assn. of America, 1948.
Kinsey, Alfred C. *Sexual Behavior in the Human Female.* Philadelphia: Sanders, 1953.
Kirkendall, Lester A. *Premarital Intercourse and Interpersonal Relationships.* New York: Matrix, 1966.

———. "Premarital Sex Relations, The Problem and Its Implications," *Pastoral Psychology* (Apr. 1956).

———. *A Syllabus and Reading Guide for Courses in Marriage and Family Relations.* Dubuque, Ia.: Brown, 1957.

Landis, Paul H. "Length of Time Required to Achieve Adjustment in Marriage," *American Sociological Review* (Dec. 1946).

———. *Making the Most of Marriage.* New York: Appleton, Century, Crofts, 1965.

———. *Understanding Teenagers.* New York: Appleton, Century, Crofts, 1955.

Laycock, Samuel R. *Brief Chats with Parents—How to Help Your Children Grow Up.* Toronto: Clark, 1956.

———. *Family Living and Sex Education.* Toronto: Baxter, 1967.

———. *Pastoral Counselling for Mental Health.* Toronto: Ryerson, 1958.

Leidy, Thomas R., and Starry, A. R. "The American Adolescent, A Bewildering Amalgam," *National Education Association Journal* (Oct. 1967).

LeMasters, E. E. *Modern Courtship and Marriage.* New York: Macmillan, 1957.

Lepp, Ignace. *The Psychology of Loving.* Baltimore: Helicon, 1963.

Lewis, C. S. *The Four Loves.* New York: Harcourt, Brace & World, 1960.

———. *The Screwtape Letters.* New York: Macmillan, 1944.

Lindgren, Henry Clay. *The Art of Human Relations.* New York: Nelson, 1953.

Lippman, Walter. "Education Versus Western Civilization," *American Scholar* (Spring, 1941).

Maltz, Maxwell. *Psycho-Cybernetics.* New York: Simon & Schuster, Essandess Special Editions, 1960.

Marshall, Catherine. *Beyond Ourselves.* New York: McGraw-Hill, Spire Books, paperback edition, 1961.

Meninger, Karl. *Love Against Hate.* New York: Harcourt, Brace, 1912.

Miles, Herbert J. *Sexual Happiness in Marriage.* Grand Rapids: Zondervan, 1967.

Morgan, Clifford. *Introduction to Psychology.* New York: McGraw-Hill, 1956.

Morgan, John Jacobs Brooks. *Keeping a Sound Mind.* New York: Macmillan, 1934.

Narramore, Clyde. *A Christian View of Birth Control.* Grand Rapids: Zondervan, 1962.

————. *How to Succeed in Family Living.* Glendale, Calif.: Regal Books, 1967.

————. *Life and Love.* Grand Rapids: Zondervan, 1956.

Ogburn, W. F., and Nimkoff, M. F. *Sociology.* Boston: Houghton Mifflin, 1940.

Olford, Stephen F. and Lawes, Frank A. *The Sanctity of Sex.* Westwood, N.J.: Revell, 1963.

Peale, Norman Vincent. *Sin, Sex, and Self-Control.* New York: Doubleday, 1965.

Polatin, Phillip and Philtine, Ellen. *Marriage in the Modern World.* New York: Lippincott, 1964.

Popenoe, Paul and Disney, Dorothy. *Can This Marriage Be Saved?* New York: Macmillan, 1960.

Reevey, William R. "Premarital Petting Behaviour and Marital Happiness Predictions," *Marriage and Family Living* (Nov. 1959).

Reik, Theodor. *Freud—Dictionary of Psychoanalysis.* Greenwich, Conn.: Premier Books, Fawcett World Library, 1963.

Rian, Edwin H. *Christianity and American Education.* San Antonio: Naylor, 1949.

Riesman, David. *The Lonely Crowd.* New Haven, Yale U., 1950.

Salisbury, H. E. *The Shook-up Generation.* New York: Harper, 1958.

Schindler, J. O. *How to Live 365 Days a Year.* Englewood, N.J.: Prentice-Hall, 1954.

————. *A Woman's Guide to Better Living 52 Weeks a Year.* Englewood, N.J.: Prentice-Hall, 1957.

Schneiders, A. A. *Personality Development and Adjustment in Adolescence.* Milwaukee: Bruce, 1960.

Shedd, Charlie. *Letters to Karen.* Nashville: Abingdon, 1965.

————. *Letters to Phillip.* Old Tappan, N.J.: Revell, 1968.

————. *The Stork Is Dead.* Waco, Tex.: Word, 1968.

Sorokin, Pitirim. *The Crisis of Our Age.* New York: Dutton, 1941.

————. *The Ways and Power of Love.* Boston: Beacon, 1954.

Steiner, Lee R. *A Practical Guide for Troubled People.* New York: Greenburg, 1952.

————. *Romantic Marriage, The Twentieth Century Illusion.* Philadelphia: Chilton, n.d.

Steiner, Heiri. *Anxiety.* New York: Visual Dell, n.d.

Strecker, Edward A. *Their Mother's Sons.* Philadelphia: Lippincott, 1951.

Suttie, Ian Dishart. *The Origins of Love and Hate.* Baltimore: Penguin Books, 1935.

Terman, Lewis. *Psychological Factors in Marital Happiness.* New York: McGraw-Hill, 1958.

Thompson, Robert. *The Psychology of Thinking.* Baltimore: Pelican Books, 1959.

Tournier, Paul. *Escape from Loneliness.* Philadelphia: Westminster, 1962.

———. *Guilt and Grace.* New York: Harper, 1962.

———. *The Meaning of Persons.* New York: Harper, 1957.

———. *A Place for You.* London: SCM, 1968.

———. *The Strong and the Weak.* London: SCM, 1963.

———. *A Whole Person in a Broken World.* New York: Harper, 1964.

Towle, Charlotte. *Common Human Needs.* New York: National Assn. of Social Workers, 1965.

Van De Velde, T. H. *The Ideal Marriage.* New York: Random House, 1930.

Wandling, A. R. *Ten Behaviour Problems Common with Pre-School Children.* House of Field, 1939.

Whalen, William. *Dollars and Sense.* St. Meinrad, Ind.: Abbey, Marriage Paperback Library, 1964.

Whiston, Lionel A. *Are You Fun to Live With?* Waco, Tex.: Word, 1968.

Wise, Carroll Alonzo. *Psychiatry and the Bible.* New York: Harper, 1956.

Young, Leontine. *Out of Wedlock.* New York: McGraw-Hill, 1954.

Index

Acceptance
  of self, 12, 13
  of others, 34, 36, 76, 121, 132, 145
Adjustments, marital, 45, 46, 65-98.
  See also Marriage and sex
  better early in marriage, 65
  of mates to children, 89, 90
  sexual, 42, 67-71
  to work pattern, 77-80
Adolescence, 141-45
  second, 107
  See also Change of life
Adoption of children, 43
Affection, 40, 41
Affections, 12, 26, 27
Aggression, 114
  excessive, 101
  in children, 114-16, 125
Alanon, 105
Alcoholic's Anonymous (A.A.), 105
Alcoholism, 100-105
Allowances, 149
Ambition
  misdirected, 28
  excessive, 28, 59
Anarchy, 184
Anger, 46
Anxiety, 18, 115, 190
Appetites, 15, 16, 26, 27
Appreciation in marriage, 56
Authoritarianism, 21, 90-92
Authority
  in the church, 189. *See also* Pastors
  conflicting with divine authority, 184.
  in the government, 183-85
  in the home. *See* Husbands; Fathers
Autonomy, 132, 134, 135, 178

Bayly, Joe, on Christian isolationism, 195
Bedwetting, 116
Behavior
  motivations of, 11, 16-18, 190
  therapy, 21
Bereavement, 162
Betrayal of Christ, 24, 28
Birth control, 42, 43

Board, payment of, 168
Bogoslavsky, B. B., on education, 131, 182
Brides, 59-62
Brothers and sisters
  in conflict, 170
  in helpful relationships, 170, 171, 206

Change of life
  female. *See* Menopause
  male, 107
Character disorder, 21
Childhood
  early, 119-20
  later, 122
  middle, 120-22
Child-raising. *See also* Discipline
  marital differences over, 90, 91
Clumsiness in adolescence, 144
Communication
  of Christianity, 190-96
  in church groups, 188
  between generations, 182, 183
  of gossip, 188
  nonverbal, 113
Companionship in marriage, 40, 59, 60
Compassion, 194, 195
Compatibility in marriage, 48, 50
Condemnation, 25
Confidences shared in marriage, 61
Conformity, 29
Conscience, 16, 21
Contentment, 79
Conversion, 29, 191, 192
Correction of children, 22. *See also* Child-raising; Discipline
Credit buying, 82, 83, 149
Criticism
  adolescent, 141, 142
  in church groups, 188
Crucifixion of Christ, 23, 24

Daydreaming, 121
Debt, 82, 83, 136, 149
Deception
  by others, 15, 16
  of self, 17, 18

220

Defrauding
  financially, 180
  immigrants, 180
  sexually, 51, 71. *See also* Sex
Demiashkevitch, Michael, on education, 181, 182
Denial of Christ by Peter, 25, 26
Dependency
  in friendship, 176, 177
  on God, 154, 155
  of grown children on parents, 86-88, 133
  in marriage, 38, 39, 102
  of parents on grown children, 87, 88, 133
  in young children, 133-35
Deprivation
  of Christ in crucifixion, 23, 24
  maternal, 113, 114
Detachment, emotional, 101
Differences
  in individuals, 66
  of male and female personality, 65-68
Discipline
  of God for His children, 202
  marital differences over, 90-93
Domination
  of children, 117, 131, 132
  in friendship, 176, 177
  of marriage partner, 101, 102
Drives
  in childhood, 115, 116
  motivating behavior, 11-14, 190
Duvall, Evelyn
  on in-laws, 87
  on premarital sex, 52

Education
  aim of, 182
  religious, 126-29
  secularization of, 183
Employers and employees, 179-81
Engagement
  broken, 34
  effect of premarital sex on, 51
Environment, 17, 20
Escape, 35
Evil, 15-17, 20, 22
Evolution, 16
Extravagance
  in husbands, 82, 83
  meaning differs with persons, 80-82
  in wives, 43, 44, 56, 81

Failure, 206, 207
  learning from, 144

Father
  God the, 204, 205
  human, 90-94, 114, 124, 168, 169
Fear. *See* Anxiety
  of remaining single, 34
Freedom, loss of, in marriage, 44, 45
Freud, Sigmund, 16
Friends
  as cause of marital conflict, 94-96
  influence of, 176, 177, 205
  need for, 175, 176
Frigidity, 67, 69. *See also* Sex in marriage
Fromm, Erich
  on dependency relationships, 176, 177
  on fatherhood, 168, 169
  on love. *See* Love
Frustration
  of oversupervised children, 114-18, 125
  of overworked wives, 61, 77-79
Fulfillment
  needed, 58, 80
  temporary loss in marriage, 45

Gluttony, 17
Goals
  in child-raising, 123-27, 146-55
  importance in mate choice, 49, 50
Gossip, 188
Grandparents, 171, 172
Gratification
  delayed, 135, 136
  needed, 117
  too much, 137
Grooms, wishes to, 56-58
Growth in marriage partners, 57, 58
Guilt, 18, 19, 20, 21, 145
  neurotic, 21
  of premarital sex, 51
  of sexual failure in marriage, 67

Homosexuality, 66, 148, 178, 193. *See also* Sex identity
Honesty, 131
  in relationships, 46, 58, 188
Horney, Karen, on neurotic drives, 190
Hostility seen in dependency relationships, 134
Housekeeping, 44, 58, 61
Humility
  false, 12, 13
  mental, 126
Husbands
  role in marriage, 45, 46, 54, 61
  weak, 60, 61
Hutterites, 21

Id, 16
Independence attained, 168
Infancy, 114-16
In-laws, 85-88, 148, 149
Integrity, 181, 194, 195
Intercourse, frequency of, 67
Isolationism, 195

Jealousy
  between siblings, 170, 171
  in the church, 186
  and crucifixion of Christ, 17
  in marriage, 60, 94-97
  neurotic, 17, 18
Josselyn, Irene, on punishment, 121, 122
Jung, Carl, on experience of awareness of identity, 134

Landis, Paul
  on in-laws, 85
  on marital adjustment, 65
  on virginity, 52
Laziness, 17
Leisure, marital conflicts over, 75, 76
Loneliness
  described by Riesman, 194
  and marriage, 36
  in urban centers, 194
  of women, 175, 176
Love
  divine, 28, 127, 200-203
  human
    characteristics of, 43, 53
    for God, 26, 27, 203
    infantile, 113
    kinds of, 200-203
    for man, 114-16
Lusts, 15-18

Marriage
  adjustments necessary in, 45, 46, 65-98
  counseling, 99-103
  defined, 47, 48
  divine guidance in, 13
  expectations, 40-44
  in later years of life, 106-10
  motivations for, 33-39
  partner, choice of, 47, 53-55
  unfaithfulness in, 98
Maturity
  defined, 123, 124
  mental, 125, 126
  physical, 124
  social, 130
  spiritual, 127, 154, 155

Menopause, 107, 108
Money, 80-83, 136, 149, 150
Moodiness in adolescence, 146
Mothering
  early, 113-16
  example of, 159-63
  overemphasized, 57
Motivations of behavior, 11-18
Mulock, Dinah Maria (Craik), on friendship, 176

Nagging
  parents, 126
  wives, 58, 59, 78, 79
Narramore, Dr. Clyde, on overactivity in the church, 188
Needs
  affiliative, 12, 22
  God-given, 13
  physiological, 11, 22
  status, 12, 13, 22
Neurosis, 21, 100, 190
  affecting marriage, 99-103
Nightmares, 116

Orgasm, simultaneous, 69, 70
Overactivity
  in business, 59, 77-80
  in the church, 45, 186-88
Overindulgence, 20, 21, 117, 118, 135-37, 202
Overprotection, 137, 169, 204
Overreaching, 50, 51

Pace, 72, 73
Parenthood
  adjustment to, 89, 90
  desire for, 42, 43
  too long delay of, 42, 43
Parents
  chosen for children in mate choice, 54, 55
  of Jesus, 167
  respect and obedience owed, 166, 167. See also Proverbs for the Space Age
Paul
  influence of, 192, 193
  an intellectual, 191
  self-conflict of, 19, 20, 22, 25
Pastors
  to be humble, 189
  to be obeyed, 189
  as counselors, 94-96
Patterns of adjustment in marriage, 85, 86

Permissiveness, 20, 21, 117, 118
Personality
    distortion of, 13, 116-18, 133
    fragmentation of, 18
Petting
    in marriage, 70
    premarital, 50, 51
Pity as a motive to marry, 37, 38
Play
    oversupervision in, 121
    purpose of, 120, 121
Polatin, Phillip
    on marriage counseling, 102, 103
    on premarital sex, 51
Possessiveness, 60
Pragmatism, 17
Preeminence
    love of, 18, 186
Pregnancy, premarital, 34, 35, 136
Prejudice, 60, 125, 126
Premature ejaculation, 69
Pride, misconception of, 12
Privacy, 131, 132
Providing for families, 43, 44
Proverbs
    on children, 123, 164
    for the Space Age, 156, 166
    on wives, 79
Psychoanalysis, 16

Quarrels
    effect on sexual response, 68
    in marriage, 45, 46

Recognition
    of children, 121
    in marriage, 40-42
    needed, 13
Relating, patterns of, 135
Religion and marriage, 48, 49, 83, 84
Repression, 117
Resentment
    in husbands, 76
    in wives, 46, 58
Respect in marriage, 53, 54
Revolt of young people, 134, 143, 144, 181, 182
Riches and marriage choice, 38, 39
Roles
    male and female, 73-75
    social, 17
Rooming-in, 114, 115

Saving, 81, 82
Security, 43, 44, 45

Self
    awareness, 205
    centeredness, 130, 131
    depreciation, 12, 13
    evaluation, 12
    identity, 12
        awareness of, 134, 135
        in marriage union, 47, 48
Sex
    development in children, 119, 120, 147, 148
    extramarital, 52
    identity, 65, 66, 147, 148. *See also* homosexuality
    male and female differences in, 67, 68
    in marriage, 42, 67-71
    as a motive to marry, 36, 37
    not necessary to individual's survival, 11
    premarital, 37, 50-53, 151-53
    unhealthy attitudes to, 70
Sibling rivalry. *See* Brothers and sisters
Sin, source of, 14-18
Sociopath, 21
Sorokin, Pitirim
    on love, 199-202
    on our society, 190
Soul union in love, 49, 50
Spending, 80-83. *See also* Money; Extravagance
Spirit, 48
Standards
    adolescent testing of, 143
    needed, 20, 22, 128
    personal establishment of, 151, 152, 153
Status needs, 12
Stealing, 131
Students, 181
Success, 13
Superego, 16
Symbiotic relationships, 177. *See also* Dependency

Tears as female emotional release, 61
Temper tantrums, 116
Temptation
    of Christ, 22, 23
    source of, of man, 16, 17
Tenderness, 59
Tensions
    from personal differences, 85, 99
    from unmet needs, 11, 12
Thumb-sucking, 116
Toilet training, 116

Tolerance, 60, 76
Transformation, 29
Trial, 162, 202
Trust in God, 154, 155

Unconscious forces, destructive, 99
    100
Unfaithfulness in marriage
    affect of, on offspring's marriage,
        96, 97
    illustrated by Hosea, 206
    an isolated incident of, 98

Values, marital differences over, 77
Virginity as best marriage prepara-
    tion, 52, 53

Vocational testing, 154

Wedding
    importance of, 52
    jitters, 55, 56
Wives
    attitude of, to husbands, 55, 169
    contradictory at times, 59
    working, 44
Work, 137, 179. *See also* Employers
    and employees
    associates at, 96, 97
    choice of, 152, 154
    overdone, 59, 77-80
    satisfactions, 136, 137